JESUS,
LIBERATION
and
LOVE

JESUS, LIBERATION and LOVE

Meditative reflections
on our believing and praying,
maturity and service

by

MARK GIBBARD
Society of St John the Evangelist, Oxford

MOWBRAY
LONDON & OXFORD

Copyright © Mark Gibbard 1982

ISBN 0 264 66550 3

First published 1982
by A. R. Mowbray & Co. Ltd
Saint Thomas House, Becket Street
Oxford, OX1 1SJ

Typeset by Memo Typography Ltd,
Nicosia, Cyprus.
Printed in Great Britain by Richard Clay
(The Chaucer Press Ltd), Bungay, Suffolk

ISBN 0-264-66550-3

CONTENTS

PREFACE

To my surprise I have been given a real 'jolt'. For a good many years I had been an active Christian, writing, travelling, lecturing, counselling. I had filled my life with plenty of work, backed up by a pattern of regular prayer. Then came this jolt—I will tell you more about it in my opening chapter—and I saw that life is not so much what I am doing for others, but what God himself has done and *is* doing in me and in them.

So God began to disturb me with his love, to 'personalise' what I was doing, and to enrich life not just with a feeling, but with a whole dimension, of *wonder*.

I was drawn to look with new eyes and heart at the basic realities behind our Christian faith, prayer and service. Much of our traditional language now seems to me tired, like old coins in need of re-minting.

So it is also to many I have talked to in all sorts of places—to some people undecided about believing, and to others who believe yet feel they are still missing an elusive 'something more'.

Many friends and writers have stimulated and encouraged me. They are woven into my life and I need them still. For I am not there yet; but already I begin to discern what could give a new unity and vigour to our lives. It is that we could actually be liberated by Love to become our true selves as we serve the world of today.

MARK GIBBARD

Michaelmas 1981
Oxford

1 THE WONDER OF BEING LOVED

By a still lake I sat on a tree stump and looked across to a college where I was teaching in Wisconsin in the midwest of the United States. The buildings, on a small hill, were usually a chilly grey, but now they glowed in the light of the setting sun. Often I took that short walk by the lake. On this day I had with me a book I was using to prepare my lectures. As I sat there alone reading, these words somehow leapt off the page at me:

> 'If when we see Jesus Christ we see God, then any previous idea we may have had of God must undergo a reconstruction which amounts to rebuilding from the basement to the coping stone.'

Time stood still. I knew I was being invited to look at Jesus with new eyes and to work out for myself what these words really implied about God and about ourselves in the contemporary world.

Perhaps you have had similar moments. They are not uncommon, but we are reticent in speaking about them; and often we don't follow them up, perhaps through pressure of other calls on our time. But I felt that this was a disclosure I must follow through; and this book is the result of my subsequent reading, reflection and prayer.

The words which so struck me were from some lectures given by Bishop Stephen Neill in Melbourne on *Christian Faith and Other Faiths*. He was commenting on a verse from John's gospel: 'He who has seen me has seen the Father'. What the New Testament tells us about Jesus seems to crystallise out in that one sentence. Stephen Neill went on to say, 'The greater part of Christian theology has been unwilling to take this tremendous affirmation as seriously as it is taken in the New Testament.'

What it amounts to for daily living is this. In the gospels

we can watch Jesus going out of his way to make contact with all sorts of men and women. He does this because he loves them; and in this way he helps them to feel understood and appreciated. This is how he puts them on the road to becoming their true selves.

Now, if when we see Jesus we see God, then it follows that God himself is always in mysterious ways trying to come into our lives, to convince us that we really matter, to help us to become our true selves. You have some idea of what it means to become your true self. I will soon say more about it. But already you see that this is something of great practical importance. The theme of this book is how you and I in our busy, complicated world can actually experience the reality of this love, which can transform us into our true selves; and how we can grasp and live in the *wonder* of what it is to be really loved in this way. This cannot be easy, but it is going to be well worth the effort.

FACING LIFE

'Being alive is being loved.' Henri Nouwen, a Dutch priest teaching at Yale and an experienced spiritual guide, has put it like that. From our own experience most of us have at least a glimpse of that truth.

As a parish priest I once called on a young couple who had had a long run of bad luck and then lost their first baby. I went as I thought to comfort them. But when I arrived I found them less distressed than I expected. So I asked the young husband, 'How are you managing to cope with everything?' He looked at me, and I shall never forget his words. 'I have my wife', he said quietly. Many of us will understand. He knew he was loved and could respond with his love. This did not take away their sorrow and their problems, but it gave them the strength they needed. Human love can do this, and so can the divine love. When we are grasped by that love which is disclosed so vividly in Jesus, we can face life and its problems with confidence.

This is why Paul can write, 'Rejoice in the Lord always; and again I will say, Rejoice'. How strange it sounds—'Rejoice always'—how all but impossible! But it is his phrase, 'in the Lord', that makes all the difference. For by those three words Paul means that God whom we see in Jesus can build up between us and himself a relationship of love, and sustain it. God intends this relationship to be as deep and mutual as the married love between that young husband and wife and quite as strengthening. We can see it actually happening in Francis of Assisi, in Mother Teresa of Calcutta and in the lives of thousands of men and women of real prayer. It could be so with us too. We arc capable of it. This is what it means when we say we are made 'in the image of God': our human nature has potentialities for a relationship of deep love with him.

Unfortunately many of us, though calling ourselves Christians or near-Christians, have not been shown how best to use this potentiality; and so, through this love, gradually to become our true selves. And yet, when this begins to happen, we mustn't expect all our difficulties to disappear. Life is seldom clear sailing. Some at least of our frustrations may remain, as they did for Paul. He had to learn to live with some handicap; he called it a 'thorn in the flesh'. But he coped. And so progressively shall we, when we are aware that we, like him, are loved with that love we see in Jesus.

THE JOURNEY OF TRUSTING

But you may well ask: 'Is all this true? Isn't there an element of wishful thinking in it? May not what you call this strength-born-of-divine-love be illusory, like a mirage in the desert? Is what you have been saying about Jesus real history?'

We must all face these questions. Personally, although I have—or am being given—a warm heart, I have a cool, critical mind. Perhaps this is partly the result of being trained as a physicist; and, when at Cambridge I changed over to theology, I did not put into cold storage my intellect or my scientific integrity. I was glad to apply them to my biblical and theological studies. I have done so ever since. My intellectual search, it is true, led me into doubt, and eventually through doubt. I found this a painful, but a purifying experience. As I look back I can now see it as providential, for it has given me a lasting fellow-feeling with those who still find it difficult to believe and to pray. It has also, I think, brought me to a faith, deeper, more modest and more mature. I can now make my own the New Testament words, 'I know who it is in whom I have trusted'.

It was in the quietness of a retreat that these words really and finally came home to me. And prayer, particularly quiet, receptive prayer, has rooted and grounded them more deeply in my mind and heart. Yet I must not give you the wrong impression, that now it is all easy going. 'My hosanna', Dostoievsky said, 'is born out of the furnace of doubt.' I myself still encounter patches of perplexity and doubt, just as I find patches of cloud among the mountains. But this hasn't stopped me from loving the mountains and tackling some stiff climbs. Nor does perplexity hold me up from trying by prayer and love to become my true self.

So let us get down to the fundamentals of believing. We begin, as Stephen Neill recommended, with Jesus. To some people what is written about Jesus seems as unreal as a fairy-tale; and many of us have moments when lurking doubts get mixed up with belief.

It always encourages me to remember that there is no need to wait for certainties in the life of believing, and especially not at the start or at a fresh beginning. 'Probability', wrote Bishop Butler, one of our greatest English theologians, 'is the very guide of life.' We can see this in the world of business. If you thought of opening a new factory or producing some new commodity, you would first employ investigators to do market research. They could never guarantee success. But if you were not prepared to make the venture on a reasonable probability, another more enterprising firm might step in and push you into bankruptcy altogether.

Again, if you set out to choose a new career for yourself, or a school for your child, or a new locality to live in, however careful the preparations, your decision would include elements of uncertainty. Even in friendship and affection, we can't begin by being sure that we shall always get on well together. We have to start with no more than probability. Then through shared experience—and sometimes chequered shared experience—our probability can grow into the deep assurance of mutual love. So it often is in our relationship of love with God.

JESUS, HISTORICAL, HUMAN, DIVINE

Then let us start with Jesus, and look in turn at his historical existence, at his humanity and, briefly, at what we call his divinity.

First, early in this century Dr Drews, a German philosopher, wrote books on the Christ myth to demonstrate, as he thought, that Jesus was no more real than the gods and goddesses of ancient Greece and Rome or of popular Hinduism, and that the stories of the gospels are merely legends prized by his hero-worshippers. This theory is now popularised by much rationalist literature in this country and by anti-religious propaganda abroad.

But in fact Jesus is pegged down into the documents of secular historians by a clear reference in Tacitus, a Latin writer, about the end of the first century AD. He described a ferocious outburst of persecution against the Christians in Rome by the Emperor Nero. Then Tacitus looked back and recorded their origin; 'Christus, from whom their name is derived, was executed at the hands of the procurator Pontius Pilate in the reign of Tiberius.'

Next, we have to ask how far we can trust the New Testament books as historical documents. I have spent a large slice of my life in this area of study and realise how inadequate anything is that I can say in a page or two. Perhaps it is useful nowadays to remind ourselves that, because these writers were followers of Jesus, they would at least intend to write honestly. Luke, for example, began his gospel by telling us that he wrote with care, and, where he could, consulted eye-witnesses of the events. This is clearly important, because it is where the gap between events and records is wide that distortions and exaggerations can creep in. In the New Testament this gap is much narrower than with most of the Old Testament books and far narrower than with nearly all the records of ancient civilisations. Paul's letters give us our earliest information about Jesus. Then the earliest evangelist, Mark, wrote probably in the sixties of the first century. Matthew's and Luke's gospels are a decade or two later. It would have been impossible in the first century to produce modern, researched biographies. Rather the gospel events and sayings are like pearls strung on a necklace. They sometimes give slightly divergent accounts. But this I think points to their general reliability rather than the opposite; for it is well known in law-courts that witnesses of some startling event often give reports which differ in detail and this in itself points to their independence and truthfulness.

Each of these gospels has been written from a particular angle; and this has led to characteristic nuances and perhaps to certain over-emphases. Matthew, for example, may have been rather more of a codifier and legalist than Jesus was himself. And John's gospel stands a little apart from the others. Archaeological research has shown that John knew well the Jerusalem of the first century. But his historical fidelity has been fruitfully married to insights into the mind and heart of Jesus, given him through long years of prayer, meditation and love.

So the gospels, apart from some easily recognisable and distinctive touches in John, present us with a wonderfully live and coherent portrait of Jesus. Even if there are details which are not strictly historical, they are certainly, as we say, 'in character'. This is what happens with the lives of nearly all great and original men. And there are many details in the gospels, so vivid and unexpected, as to be certainly authentic. 'Look at him! a glutton and a drinker, a friend of scoundrels and prostitutes' (Luke 7.34)—who would have invented that comment about any religious figure?

Dr C. H. Dodd, one of the most distinguished New

Testament scholars, has written: 'The gospels together give so consistent, so coherent, so distinctive a picture of Jesus, as to be beyond human invention.' He went on to say that the whole of Jesus' sayings recorded in the gospels have so unmistakable a stamp that they cannot possibly be only the compilation of early Christian teachers' adaptations of his words. Rather, Dr Dodd concluded: 'They have the ring of originality. They betray a mind whose processes were swift and direct, hitting the nail on the head without waste of words.'

Secondly, let us next glance at the real *humanness* of Jesus. Often Christian authors have, through a distorted kind of reverence, not done justice to Jesus' complete humanness. How well, for example, Jesus knew what utter exhaustion feels like. Once he was so tired that he slept in a small boat through a storm so fierce that life-long fishermen were scared for their lives. Also Jesus' love was real. It was not vague kindness towards everyone. It was personal love focussed on particular men and women to meet their actual situation: the beggar Bartimaeus, for example, who for Jesus was not a blind man lost in a crowd; or that rich young man, whom Jesus freely let go away from him although he had a special affection for him (Mark 10.46-52, 17-22). We shall see the' importance of this humanity of Jesus all through this book and specially in the chapter about becoming our true selves.

Then thirdly, people have sensed in Jesus not only his humanity, but also something beyond, something divine. 'Who then is this?', they kept on asking. Jesus seems usually to have been reticent about himself, because his main task was to make God and his kingdom real to others. Yet Jesus saw himself as man and more than man. We can find plenty of evidence of this in our earliest records of his life. Let me quote one instance from the earliest gospel, the well-authenticated parable of the vineyard (Mark 12.1-12).

God the lord of the vineyard sends, one after another, his servants, his messengers, to collect the harvest of grapes. But the local workers in the vineyard drive these

15

servants off; some they beat up, some they kill. All the people listening to Jesus see that these servants stood for God's prophets, the most inspired of men, like Hosea and Jeremiah. And then God says, 'I'll send no more prophets; I'll send someone in an entirely different category.' In this way Jesus himself tells us that he is not just one more inspired man, but one who has a relationship so unparalleled with God that when we look at him, we see what God is like.

John, when he writes later in the first century, focusses Jesus' meaning in that luminous sentence: 'He who has seen me has seen the Father'.

JESUS' DISCLOSURE OF GOD'S LOVE TODAY

When we watch Jesus, we see God. I would like to try to spell that out. But before doing so let us glance at a great difficulty many people find in accepting this truth. When they look at life, it doesn't seem to them as if we are loved by God; nor does it to us in our worst moments. The world seems too full of tragedy for that—like a sky covered by impenetrable cloud: suffering caused by earthquakes, drought, injustice, cruelty; and, more personally, illness or loss, anxiety about our friends and families, problems of work or money, fears for the future. Seeing and knowing such pain and misery, people say, 'How can there be a God, a God of love?' Yet even on the blackest days, if we can take the New Testament into our hands, there we shall see a beam of sunlight piercing through those terrible black clouds. It makes us sure that behind the darkness there must be light, warmth, love, the One whom we call God. And—you have realised—Jesus in the gospels is this revealing beam.

Jesus' way of loving then is God's way of loving now. God's love for us, like Jesus' love, is available at any minute. It does not always begin by challenging us. It seeks us and it never deserts us. We see from the gospels that it is love which knows how to meet us where we are.

Nicodemus comes to Jesus at night, when no one will

16

know about it. He is a typically thoughtful man, who, like many today, doesn't quickly accept new ways of looking at life and certainly doesn't wish to identify himself with what may be only a passing popular religious mood. Jesus welcomes him at once; he doesn't hint that Nicodemus might have come at a more convenient time. Soon they are in no conventional talk, but in a conversation which touches the real issues of life.

Then Jesus, tired and thirsty after walking miles under the eastern sun, sits by a wall at Samaria. I know that deep well; it is the only one in the district. A woman comes with her water-jar. Jesus intuitively senses what kind of woman she is. She has had a succession of husbands and is now living with another man. Jesus knows that according to strict convention he ought not to talk alone with a woman, especially he, a rabbi, with such a woman as this—and a Samaritan. Later on, when Jesus' disciples come and see them, they are shocked at this breach of convention. Jesus doesn't begin by probing into her situation. He only asks for a little cold water. Then he knows how to let the conversation run its course; yet skilfully he brings her to understand her true self and her need of the real God, whom he discloses to her.

At another time, Jesus' human understanding led him to take more of an initiative. Zacchaeus was a typical unscrupulous tax-collector of those days; he had piled up a good deal of money for himself. Out of mere curiosity he thought he would like to see what sort of man this Jesus was. So he climbed up a tree in a Jericho street to have a better view of Jesus. Then to his complete surprise Jesus stopped under the tree, looked up and said, 'Zacchaeus, I'd like to see your home.' Just how the conversation went that day we do not know; but in his sensitivity and love Jesus helped Zacchaeus to see how he could make reparation to those he had cheated. Zacchaeus began to find his true self that day.

But perhaps for some of us our Lord's love for Peter discloses the kind of sustaining care we need. Like Peter we have our ups and downs, alternately over self-confident and then depressed. Peter had his high moments, his sense of wonder in Jesus' presence on the mountain of transfiguration and his intuition at Caesarea Philippi that in some unique way Jesus was the Son of the living God. But Peter had also his bad moments. Once when he tried to dissuade Jesus from going up to face the plots of his opponents in Jerusalem, Jesus turned on him with a withering rebuke (Mark 8.31-33). Jesus loved him too much to be soft with him. Then, on the night before the crucifixion, Peter's nerve quite failed and he denied he was in any sense a follower of Jesus. A little later on in that night of despair, Jesus in his love caught Peter's eye, and Peter burst into tears.

Jesus never gave up caring for Peter; nor will God ever, whatever we may do, whether we forget or even defy him, give up caring for us. So after the resurrection Jesus took the initiative and asked Peter if he really loved him after all. When Peter assured him he did, Jesus entrusted other people to Peter's care. For people can be securely entrusted to our care only when we are aware that we are loved by God and are responding in love—for then it is that we shall neither spoil them nor dominate them, but shall be trying to love them with the kind of love we see in Jesus.

And we shall retain a sense of *wonder* that we are really loved by God. This will not be just an intellectual conviction, nor only an emotional experience. It will be something rooted and grounded in our personality. It may often be paradoxically 'too deep to be felt', but it will overflow into concern and love for others.

This happens to quite ordinary people. I used to notice it in Madeleine Delbrêl, a social worker, whom I knew towards the end of her life in a poor quarter of Paris. She was the only daughter of a railwayman; but as a girl she was interested in music and art, and she had a book of her poems published. She was a lapsed Catholic. After a long intellectual struggle, she came back to faith and then to prayer. 'In reading and reflecting', she said, 'I have found God, but in praying I believe God found me.' She never in her tightly-packed life lost her natural gaiety nor the wonder of being found and loved by God. 'Radiant', people always called her, *'une éblouie de Dieu'*. She kept open house; her telephone seemed always to be ringing; she couldn't follow any convent-like timetable of prayers. Her going into the desert retreat for prayer was, she used to say, 'a journey of five stations on the metro at the end of the day.'

Perhaps we could pause now, dwell for a minute or two on the reality of God and his love, and put into words our hopes and our needs as we set out to discover our true selves in everyday life at greater depth. Some prayer like this may help us to start:

> We wish to be quiet and still.
> Help us to see in our daily lives something more
> than things and events;
> Help us to recognise something yet more in those
> whose lives touch ours.
> And in this something yet more make us sensitive
> to a reality which is more than human,
> aware of a love from beyond,
> a love we see fully in Jesus,
> a love which begins to draw us to Abba, our
> God.

2   GOD AS HE REALLY IS

A disclosure came to Blaise Pascal, the mathematician. We can still see at his birthplace at Clermont-Ferrand in the Auvergne his *machine arithmétique*, as he called it, designed on the same essential lines as today's computers.

On Monday, 23 November 1654 he was sitting in the evening at his home in Paris, reading the seventeenth chapter of John's gospel. Then at half-past ten there was given to him quite unexpectedly a disclosure of God and his love. He took up his pen and wrote quickly in slanting letters:

God of Abraham, God of Isaac, God of Jacob, not of
                        the philosophers and scholars.
Certitude. Certitude. Feeling. Joy. Peace.
God of Jesus Christ,
My God and thy God.

Pascal resolved to keep this disclosure ever in his mind and heart; so he sewed the paper into the lining of the jacket he always wore; and there it was discovered when he died. We too need to treasure our disclosures, though few of them, of course, are so dramatic as Pascal's. My own, by that lake in Wisconsin, was in manner far more low key but in substance the same.

Up to then my faith, which had been a great strength to me in my life and ministry, had been fundamentally a belief in God as creator and lawgiver, the God of the astronomers and moralists; and then I had fitted Jesus the revealer and redeemer into that rather cerebral framework.

But from that day by the lake I knew that I had to respond in a fresh way with heart and mind to Jesus himself—and so come to discover God as he really is. The Carmelite, Ruth Burrows, has put very clearly the change I then needed to make and which I think many Christians still need to make: 'Instead of looking at Jesus to learn what God is like and how we go to God, we had projected on to Jesus our own ideas of God and so had lost sight of Jesus and his essential message.'

Yet I must not leave you with a misleading impression of the change that has come into my life. I still enjoy reading in a busy life as much as I can of the philosophers, the moralists and the poets; and I love the psalms, the prophets and the treasures of the Old Testament as much as ever. But now Jesus is the heart of it all. And in a fresh sense it all points to and converges on him. For it is Jesus himself who supremely discloses to us both God and his unalterable love—and also incidentally discloses who men and women really are. This double disclosure has brought to me, as it did to Pascal, certitude and joy in my reflecting and praying these last few years—though not always clarity.

POINTERS TO GOD THROUGH OBSERVATION AND REASONING

That has been my own experience; yet God comes into people's lives in many other, different ways—probably in almost as many ways as there are seekers and believers. And in every age some philosophers, men of science, moralists and historians have pointed men and women along the road towards the reality of God. Perhaps, without them, Pascal himself would not have had this later, great disclosure. So let us look briefly in turn at three of the signposts they provide for us—in the observation of nature, in the ethical character of man, and in the fact of religious experience.

First, in *the world of nature* Paul said he could perceive God's 'eternal power and deity' (Rom. 1.20). We today might put it differently. Our scientists seem able to detect in nature regular sequences and patterns. Future positions of stars can be forecast because they move in a regular way. Eclipses are accurately predicted and comets dated. Even in tiny insignificant creatures we observe an intricate life-cycle. And we can see in the evolutionary

21

process now more or less universally accepted that, in spite of some strange dead ends, there is a remarkable continuous development from inanimate matter right up to man as we know him, to *homo sapiens*.

Faced with careful observations like these, as reasoning creatures we feel bound to ask: 'Why this orderliness? Why the consistency? Why such pattern? Why such a development?' And our reason submits: either it's all mere coincidence or there is behind it some kind of purpose, some kind of designing. The latter to me seems much the more likely. So in the observation of nature I and others find the signpost and impetus we need in our search for God.

A second signpost comes, as I see it, from the observation of *the ethical character of man*. It impressed the philosopher Immanuel Kant. This signpost towards God is not as simply discerned as some might think at first sight. It needs to be thought about carefully. It is this: many people are at times conscious within themselves of a sense of right and wrong; that is, they are convinced that a certain act is right and so ought to be done, even if it makes them unpopular or brings great hardship on them; and they are equally sure that another action is wrong and so ought not to be done, even though it would never be found out.

Yet anthropologists show us how ideas of right and wrong diverge among different peoples. And we see also for ourselves how from generation to generation these ideas can change with further knowledge and experience. Yet these variations do not invalidate our main point. The similar fact that people's tastes for particular foods differ and also change with the years does not alter the reality of their basic hunger. So the fact that people's personal ideas about some moral questions change does not alter the reality of the basic distinction of right and wrong in their consciences.

Some people have tried to explain away this sense of right and wrong as entirely the result of social conditioning. But this cannot be so, when we see Socrates, William Wilberforce and so many others persevering in what their conscience required of them in complete defiance of the social assumptions of their age. Nor can this inner sense of right and wrong be adequately accounted for by psychology. It is true that psychology can show us something of the process by which these ethical convictions are built up; but psychology itself, because of the self-imposed limitations of its field of study, cannot judge the value of these convictions nor say what ultimate reality is behind them. A parallel may make this clearer. A doctor can explain why without food we are hungry. But he cannot by his medical knowledge tell us whether there is food in the cupboard to satisfy our hunger or not.

Therefore many careful observers of ethical behaviour have thought and still think that there is some unknown factor, some supreme source of moral insight and power within us, leading us on. I agree with them. So this is for me a second signpost.

The third is *spiritual experience*. Millions all over the world have claimed that through prayer—in a wide sense of that word—they have encountered the reality of God. I do not refer to exceptional experiences. Rather I mean, for example, a sense of the presence of God, or a sense that God takes hold of some events in our lives and in his wisdom and love shapes and reshapes them. We may see this clearly among the great men and women of prayer, like the apostle Paul or Mother Julian of Norwich or William Temple. But these things are not uncommon, they occur in the lives of many ordinary people.

Of course, some people may have been mistaken or deluded in prayer, just as others think they are in love, when they are not—but this does not prove that all love or most love is a delusion. And men and women of real prayer, like Dietrich Bonhoeffer or Evelyn Underhill, do not look like victims of delusion; rather they were people of balanced character and acute intellect.

Although strange and fanatical things have sometimes been done by men of prayer, yet on balance immensely good things have come through prayer. One impressive example out of many comes to my mind from the Jewish faith. A thousand years or so before Christ the Jewish people were, it seems, much like the Semitic tribes around them; they thought there were many gods, and they themselves were excessively preoccupied about details of worship and sacrifice, and far too little concerned about social justice and integrity. The complete redirection of the Jewish people from these primitive and misguided ways came through a remarkable succession of men of prayer between about 750 and 550 BC, like Amos, Micah and Isaiah, whom we call 'prophets'. They all claimed that through prayer they were in living contact with the real God; and that he gave them the strength to meet head-on the entrenched opposition of their rulers and of the 'official' church. It was through the influence of these prophets that the Hebrew nation accepted a firm belief in one God of a kind unparalleled in the ancient world, and came to give their loyalty to this One God who cared above all for honesty, love and mercy. This is only one example of the vital power of religious experience, which seems to me to be the third signpost pointing to the reality of God.

These three signposts are only pointers. They compel no one. But they invite us to explore in this direction. I grant there are problems, like that of suffering and evil, which I mentioned in the previous chapter. But this search is not anti-rational. It goes in the same *direction* as observation and reason. It is like the step of inquiring confidence which leads us from mere acquaintance with one another into human friendship and love. As we take this step, sometimes diffidently, we often have a sense, perhaps faint at first, of the presence of Him who said to Pascal, 'You would not be seeking me, unless you had already found me.'

WHAT KIND OF GOD?

But what kind of God encounters us? Perhaps not the kind of God we might have expected from what some of us were told when we were young. He is not a rather severe, legally-minded God, watching to catch us out; far from it.

Still less is he an 'impersonal' force behind the universe and behind the evolutionary process. For as he is our originator and maker, he must be 'personal', or else he would be less than we are as human persons, less rich in potentialities than we are. Yet when we say he is 'personal', we don't imagine he is just man writ large; what we mean most of all is this, that he and ourselves are potentially capable of deep personal relationships.

God is not only transcendent, but also immanent; that is, as Paul says, God is not only over all, he is *in* all things (Eph. 4.6). 'His strong heart stirs the ever-beating sea.' The personalities of our friends come over to us largely through their bodies, of which some parts, like sparkling eyes, are more particularly expressive. So God, who is in all things, conveys something of himself in very *varying* ways through creation and through the course of events, at least to those whose eyes have been opened. It is wanting to share all this truth with you that has made me write this book.

But here perhaps a difficulty crosses our mind—or rather our imagination. Doesn't the size of the universe, shown by modern astronomy, mean that God, even if he is personal, must be beyond close relationships with such infinitesimal beings as ourselves? I don't think so. We are just letting our imagination become mesmerised by astronomical figures. We are forgetting, it seems, that we are specially 'made in his image', that is capable of communion with him. In effect we are still imagining God as the remote controller of the universe, preoccupied with stars and nebulae, with no time to wonder at the love of men and women. But whatever God is, he is not that. The Bible and contemporary theologians make that clear. What matters most to God is not size— whether Mount Everest or a giant star—but response, the human response of love. That is what really matters both for you and for God—God as he really is, disclosed in Jesus.

The God whom we are trying to seek with the

scientists, philosophers and scholars has more than responded to our seeking. He has in his love come to meet us through the lives and words of men he has inspired, particularly of the Jewish faith, Abraham, Isaac, Jacob, Moses and Isaiah—and above all he has come to us, as we have seen, in Jesus—and not chiefly through Jesus' words but through his personality, his life, his death, his being raised again so as to be *inseparably with us* and within us.

The love that is at the heart of Christian praying and living is, as the New Testament says, not our loving God, but fundamentally his loving us. Even if we cannot always feel this love, we can always see it in his coming to us in Jesus. We become increasingly aware of his immense love for us; his love awakens in us a response of love for him; and then this love, as it deepens, reaches out more and more into love to others.

JESUS DISCLOSES WHO GOD IS

So if we wish to know God as he actually is, let us then, as Stephen Neill recommends, fix our eyes on Jesus. We cannot know as much about Jesus as we would like. But one thing we are certain of is that the heart of his life, what made him 'tick', was his meeting with and responding to God's love through prayer.

Nowadays we often think of prayer as something baffling or dull or commonplace. But when Jesus prayed it was something startlingly new. That is why one of his followers asked him, 'Lord, teach us how to pray'. All their lives these men had prayed. They had grown up in a society with an intense faith in God. Yet they sensed that there was something quite unprecedented in Jesus' praying. And the heart of it was enshrined in one word from his mother-tongue, *Abba*. When Jesus' sayings were translated from his Aramaic into Greek, the *lingua franca* of the world of his day, the first Christians sometimes left this word untranslated—and with good reason. A German scholar, Dr Joachim Jeremias, has examined the prayers of the Jews at that time with minute care. They usually addressed God with elaborate titles, but never as Abba. This word was not the ordinary Aramaic word for Father; it was the child's first word 'Daddy', for his father. So Dr Jeremias says of Jesus' use of Abba in his prayer: 'It was something new, something unique and unheard of that Jesus dared to take this step and to speak with God as a child speaks with his father simply, intimately, securely.' But grown-up sons and daughters also used this word with the feeling of 'My dear Father'. Jesus prayed to Abba as a mature man when he faced his agony in the garden of Gethsemane.

What then does the Abba prayer disclose to us about God as he really is? And what does it say about Jesus' consequent relation to him? It reveals a deep relationship of certitude, intimacy and confidence.

Abba speaks of Jesus' utter *certitude*, his sureness about God, something difficult for many of us now to realise after two hundred years of scepticism from David Hume onwards in the west. This inner sureness can only come to us as a gift, as it came to Pascal; it is like the gift of love; and how much we need day by day to pray for these two intimately linked gifts. Yet we should not feel discouraged if the gift of certitude is not always given us. 'Faith is not security away from darkness', Archbishop Michael Ramsey wrote. 'It is the will to go on with darkness all around.' Let us remember that even for Jesus this sureness was clouded over in his hour of darkness on the cross. Those terrible words of his, 'Eli, Eli, lama sabachthani?', 'My God, my God, why hast thou forsaken me?', have paradoxically been a comfort to me in my times of doubt and perplexity. Awareness of the reality of God was not always easy even for Jesus.

Abba also reveals to us Jesus' *intimacy* with the Father. It tells us of a God who is 'ever close', as another German scholar, Dr Bultmann, has put it. This can be so too for us. But, as Dr Bultmann goes on to say, 'The decision of faith is never final, it needs constant renewal in every fresh situation.' This was as true for Jesus as it is for us. It was as Jesus turned so frequently to God that his own intimacy with him was renewed. He looked, for example, to the Father with trust and self-offering before he fed the five thousand.

In passing let us notice that we do not necessarily have to use the word Father to express our intimacy with God. Some people would find it difficult to do so; for to them the word Father has no warm resonance, because they have not experienced the deep affection of a human father. But the scriptures themselves show that we can also come to God as a close friend. Further, as we shall see later, the New Testament describes the Christian fellowship, in which we are personally called to share, as Christ's bride. In fact our intimate relationship with God is potentially so deep and rich that we need many complementary images to convey it. Eventually we may find that its intimacy, marvel and wonder will become too profound for any imagery to be adequate.

This intimacy led Jesus—and can lead us—both to *confidence* in praying and also to courage in living. When Jesus prays, he prays with confidence—confidence in his Father himself, not confidence in prayer as a technique. 'I thank you, Father, that you hear me. I know that you always hear me.' (John 11.42). Indeed it is this confidence in praying that leads to courage in living. Professor Dodd wrote of this love-inspired confidence which is crystallised in the word Abba: 'Here is to be found the driving force and source of energy for an almost impossible mission, here certainly the source of the inflexible resolution with which he went, knowingly, to death in the service of his mission.'

Jesus prayed with confidence not only for himself but also for others. He prayed for himself that he might have courage to fulfil God's purpose and calling for him. We see in the darkness of Gethsemane what a struggle Jesus' prayer sometimes was—and so sometimes ours may be—that he might follow God's way for him, the road of the cross. It was this road that made him the channel of God's forgiveness, liberation and love for many.

In Jesus, confident petition for himself fans out into confident intercession for others. In the pattern prayer which he gave us, the Lord's prayer, he asks us always to pray in the plural, never for ourselves alone. Our prayer, like his, is to be as wide as the world. For the whole world is God's world. 'Thy kingdom come on earth as it is in heaven.' Yet there is nothing vague about Jesus' intercession. Jesus loves personally and prays personally. He prays individually and confidently. 'Simon, Simon, for you have I prayed that your faith may not fail.' Jesus foresaw that Peter's loyalty to him would be tested in that night before Good Friday. Jesus had more than an inkling that the way of prayer, like the way of love, would not always run smoothly. Yet Jesus continued to pray with confidence. 'I have prayed that when you have come to yourself, you will lend strength to your brothers' (Luke 22.31-32).

OUR PARTICIPATION IN THE ABBA PRAYER OF JESUS

God's love disclosed in Jesus involves the reconstruction from foundation to coping stone not only of our knowledge and experience of God, but also of the way we see and experience life—often starting from the way in which we pray.

One day at prayer Jesus 'exulted in the Holy Spirit'. Jesus knew too the exultation and wonder of praying. Then he thanked God that not only did the Father know him intimately and he knew the Father in the same way, but also that he could disclose the Father to his followers, so that *they could know the Father as intimately as he did* (Luke 10.21-22). So Jesus imparts to them and to us his own love-rooted confidence in the Father, or, as Joachim Jeremias puts it, Jesus allows us to 'participate in his own communion with God.'

We receive this gift of loving, confident prayer, not through our own tense efforts to pray, but through being quiet, receptive, open to the Spirit. As Paul himself put it, 'God has sent into our hearts the Spirit of his Son, saying Abba, Father' (Gal. 4.6). As we learn step by step to be more open to the Spirit of Jesus, we shall experience—though probably not without setbacks—something of the certitude, the intimacy, the confidence and courage which Jesus had. This will mean discipline, perseverance, suffering. Even then we shall experience this progress not as our achievement, but as God's gift. Paul goes so far as to say that through this Spirit-inspired prayer, Abba, we become partners with Jesus, fellow-children of God with Jesus, so that to us Jesus 'is the eldest among a large family of brothers' (Rom. 8.29).

We too shall become with Jesus channels of God's love, through our loving, our serving and our praying for others. This praying for others will not be vague, but 'personalised' as Jesus' praying was for Peter. Indeed our praying for them will be our personal collaboration with God and with his love for them. We shall be doing for them what those men did in the gospel story for their paralysed friend, when they carried him on a stretcher along the crowded road and let him down through the mud roof of the house where Jesus was. There was no other way of bringing him to Jesus for forgiveness and healing, and they were so eager and concerned to do it.

Jesus shows us not only who God actually is; he also shows us the true selves that we could with his love become. But before we go on to that, we might pause and reflect quietly on the beginnings of our new discovery. 'All the troubles of life come upon us', Pascal also said, 'because we refuse to sit quietly at home for a while each day.'

> 'Commune with your own heart and be still.'
> 'God of Jesus Christ,
> My God and thy God.'
> Help me to be with you in quiet confidence.
> I wish to discover life at greater depth.
> I am concerned not only for myself,
>   but also for those who are near to me,
>   and for all our fellow-seekers.
> Help me to give myself more trustingly to you,
>   although I do not yet quite see what this involves,
> so that you can use me, my concern, my loving,
>   my praying to help them.
> Show us how to become our true selves
>   and to discover what life really can become.

3 BECOMING OUR TRUE SELVES

I would like this book to be down-to-earth and practical, a book about things that actually happen. When God's love in Jesus becomes central to our lives, things do happen; first, because in Jesus God really meets us; and secondly because in Jesus we discover *who* we are on the way to becoming, our true selves, men and women in the true humanness which God intended for us.

These things can happen anywhere, because God in Christ is everywhere. But they happen at special times and places—as I have seen myself—like Taizé the home of an ecumenical Christian community. Taizé is a mere dot on the map, a single village street of apricot-coloured stone cottages, climbing up a hill from which you have a glorious view of the rolling hills of Burgundy patched with woods and vineyards, wheat-fields and meadows. Yet the other Easter forty thousand young people came and camped around, and why? Because they felt they would be understood and appreciated there.

This is a community at whose heart is the love of God in Jesus. Its rule says to each member, 'Give yourself each day to Christ', and equally, 'Open yourself to all that is human, be really present in the world as it is.' The second of these qualities has spread to the community from Frère Roger, its founder and inspirer. He has told us of a particular moment of disclosure and insight, when this quality began to take root in him: 'There came a day—I can remember the date and I could describe the place—when the subdued light of a late summer evening was settling down to a darkness over the countryside. That day I made a resolution. I said: "I will begin with myself and try to understand myself, and then I will commit myself to trying to understand everyone whom I meet." That day I knew that resolution was final and would last until I die. Life consists of simply returning again and again for the rest of my days to that once-and-for-all resolution to seek to understand each one.' I see a link between his experience and mine beside that lake in Wisconsin. For since that day I have gradually come to see not only God quite differently, but also the people round me as my brothers and sisters on the road to becoming their true selves, disclosed in Jesus.

THE SEARCH FOR OUR TRUE SELVES

Before we go further, I would like to speak about two preliminary matters. The first is how I am speaking of self in *three* senses—our actual present self, our exterior self and our future true self. I do not mean that these three are quite distinct from one another. They are mysteriously interwoven. There is, first, our present self as it actually now is, deep within us; if we try, we can find out something, but by no means all, about it. Next, there is the exterior self, which we show to the world, what the Geneva psychiatrist Paul Tournier calls our 'personnage'. This exterior 'put-on' self hinders real friendships and close relationships; although it may have its place in professional life and is sometimes a necessary protective measure, for we cannot always wear our hearts on our sleeves. Then, there is our true inner self, the particular self whom God intends that we should become. We are all *on the road* towards becoming our true selves and want to be further along it; or in the words of Browning:

> Man is not yet
> But wholly hopes to be....

You may wonder whether this maturing into our true selves is the same thing as finding and fulfilling our vocation, the particular calling to which we believe God is leading us. Not quite, I would say; but they are close. Paul was great in his vocation as an apostle. But more fundamentally he was great as a man in his relationship of love and trust towards God and towards the men and

32

women he met. It was because of *who* he became that he was great in his calling and life-work as an apostle.

The second preliminary matter I would like to mention is the great value of speaking, as I have done these last few years, of the aim of the Christian life as *becoming our true selves*. Some people might hesitate about this and ask: 'Isn't this very different from the more traditional description of our aim in life as doing our duty to God and our neighbour, or living to the glory of God?' They might even go on to say: 'Doesn't "becoming our true selves" sound rather like polite self-indulgence? Aren't we in danger of becoming a bit "soft" with ourselves?'

We shall soon see that so far from being a self-indulgence, the road to becoming our true selves is a steep one, though the steepness does not daunt us because we are drawn on by love. There are also on this road great obstacles, outside and *within* us, which we cannot overcome by selfconscious effort alone. Nor is seeking to become our true selves a 'self-culture', like some forms of transcendental meditation; because, as Niebuhr says, 'Self does not realise itself fully, when self-realisation is our conscious aim.'

Next, trying to do our best in the service of our neighbour really requires that we leave behind our old self as it is and press on towards our new true self. This is, I think, what Paul Tournier means when he says, 'I must ask God daily to liberate me from myself so that I may be put at the disposal of others.' Further, maturing into our true selves is in fact pleasing to God, for we are becoming what he has always intended us to be and so glorifying him. Irenaeus of Lyons in the second century said: *Gloria enim Dei vivens homo*—'For the glory of God is man fully alive.'

How then do we mature into our true selves? Not by 'working on ourselves' but by growing in true love to God and to others. John Mann, a Benedictine, says, 'We only become our true selves, when we are wholly turned towards another.' We have to find our own way in this double love. God will give us his light. We can learn also from the experience of those who have gone before us. But their time is not our time. There was only one Francis of Assisi; there can't be another. What disasters I have seen when people model themselves on someone else. We must not even try to imitate Jesus literally. You will notice that when the New Testament speaks of imitating, 'Be ye imitators of God', it means the internal assimilation of love: 'And walk *in* love, as Christ loved us' (Eph. 5.1-2). To copy Jesus externally would make us narrow, archaic—and scrupulous as well. Besides, it might only make us feel hopeless and discouraged. Jesus was never intended to be just an example; much more he is our source of strength and love to draw us on, so that we can grow step by step into his likeness—and into our true selves. So an Indian poet wrote:

> I saw my Lord with my heart's eye
> And I said, 'Who art thou, Lord?'
> 'Thyself', he replied.

GROWING INTO CHRIST

The fundamental thing about Jesus is that he knew he was loved by his Father, Abba, ever present; he loved the Father in return, and this love overflowed on to those around him. It is into this love that we are called to grow today. We grow, as we have seen, not by imitating him externally, but by letting ourselves be loved by God in Jesus—and through others. Friendship changes us. Jesus calls us his friends; and he is not just the Jesus of past history, he is the living Jesus, our contemporary ever with us. This means prayer and prayer in which we are really open to him.

But we shall never come truly close to him only by praying, however well and however long we pray. Like all friendship and love, we need not only to talk together, but to grow together, to grow into one. So the New Testament calls us 'to grow up fully into Christ', 'to attain to mature manhood, measured by nothing less than the full stature of Christ' (Eph. 4.13, 15).

Yet some people are rather afraid of this closeness with the Lord, as they are sometimes, understandably, afraid of a close human love. They are afraid of being dominated, absorbed, even swamped by their friend or partner. But in *real* friendship and love we do not de-individualise one another. On the contrary. 'In love we set one another free to become our real selves', as Daniel Day Williams puts it in his *Spirit and the Forms of Love*. And this is certainly true about God's loving us: God does not want us to be cool nonentities; he wants us to grow into our rich, diverse humanness.

How warm and outgoing Jesus was! Would you like to make a list for yourself of the things in Jesus which particularly strike you? I do not mean so much his outward actions as his inner qualities. And how could these qualities help us to mature into our true new selves? Let me tell you what has impressed me as I have tried to look at Jesus with new eyes.

The first thing—and I can't help saying it again, it is so much part of him—is that *particular, inner spring of love*, which inspired him to go out to meet, to make real contact with, to understand, to encourage, so many kinds of people. The New Testament word for it is *agape*. It is not only what we feel deeply, nor even what we actually do to love and to care for others; this love is reality, the supreme, inner reality. For God *is* love; love is not only something he does; love is what he is. And Jesus discloses this love, eternal, unalterable, coming to every individual, however evil or useless he may feel himself to be. And how does Jesus disclose and bring to us this divine love? Through his human loving. His human love is the visible and tangible sign that, like a sacrament, brings God's love to us. In response to it we are called and enabled to love God and love our neighbours.

Our human friendship and love *can*—wonder of wonders—convey sacramentally God's love to others, as Jesus' love did. But it can easily fall below this way of loving. We know this and so does the New Testament, which uses other Greek words for love. There is *philia* for the affection of friends and comrades; and *epithemia* and other words for lust, possessive or irresponsible. Another word, *eros*, not found in the Greek Testament, is used for strong, genuine human love and also for the love of all that is beautiful and true. It often did not carry that debased ring which our word 'erotic' sometimes has. Indeed Ignatius, the bishop of Antioch and martyr early in the second century, almost certainly wrote of Jesus as 'my *eros*'. But Anders Nygren, a Lutheran theologian, wrote a book, *Agape and Eros*, which set these two loves in very sharp contrast. It had a great vogue, in spite of criticisms from some New Testament theologians, and had an unfortunate influence on my generation of students. On the other hand Paul Tillich wrote: 'If *eros* and *agape* cannot be united, *agape* towards God is impossible.' For *eros* can be a hidden dynamo of controlled energy in our loving both God and our neighbour. This is the kind of vigour which, firstly, I see in Jesus' love.

And his love was always focussed love. Perhaps the words about Jesus the good shepherd, his knowing each one of his sheep—and each one individually knowing him—have become rather commonplace, tired language. They regained their force for me when D. T. Niles, an ecumenical leader in Sri Lanka, told me in his old age of a conversation he had with a simple Tamil shepherd who could neither read nor count. 'How', asked D. T. (as everyone called him), 'do you know that all your sheep are there, if you can't count them?' The shepherd replied, 'I don't need to count them; I know them; so if one is not there, I miss that one.' So Jesus' love and attention is directed to each individual and his particular needs at that moment—to the despairing man, crippled for thirty-eight years, by the pool of Bethesda; and to Jairus, the leading man from the synagogue, whose twelve-year-old daughter was at death's door; while to the children who were brought to him he gave a good hug—that is what Mark says. And this is the kind of loving which Jesus inspires in those who live close to him—in Francis de Sales, Madeleine Delbrêl, Brother Roger of Taizé

The second thing which strikes me about Jesus is his *deep fidelity*. Jesus both enjoys his friendships and keeps them going. When he and his disciples had been very busy, he said, 'Come, let us get into a boat and go off and have a picnic.' He loved Martha and Mary and Lazarus, and enjoyed staying in their home at Bethany. He allowed Mary Magdalene, Joanna, Susanna and other women to go about the country with him and his disciples and help them, though the strict rabbis probably disapproved of this. The rabbis also objected to Jesus' taking meals with prostitutes and scoundrels of tax-collectors; and he did this because he enjoyed their company, not to set an example of 'broadmindedness'.

Yet, when his friends were awkward and quarrelled with one another, he didn't walk out and leave them. And, as we have seen, when Peter tried to persuade Jesus to avoid the suffering which his life's mission was bringing on him, Jesus reproved him severely. When it was necessary, Jesus was prepared to risk a row. He could speak the truth, the unpopular truth, just because he loved with such fidelity. We see what it involves to grow into our true selves.

Thirdly, I see in Jesus a man of great gifts, who has *developed his gifts* for the joy and service of others. He had a gift for friendship and love; but he had to learn how to use it wisely to encourage others to grow into their true selves. He had a remarkable ability for speaking; but he had to perfect that skill to tell those gems of parables and aphorisms.

You will recall the story Jesus told of a master who entrusted various sums of money to his servants to use while he went on a journey. On his return the only man he reprimanded was the one who had done absolutely nothing wrong. This man handed his master's money safely back; he had not wasted a penny. To his great surprise he was severely reprimanded for his cautiousness (Matt. 25.14-29).

I ask myself why we, Jesus' friends, often don't develop the gifts he has given us—gifts of prayer and of friendship and other skills. It may be indolence. It may be fear of someone saying to us, when we do not succeed, 'There, I told you, you'd never manage it!' Or it may be we have not kept our priorities right. I knew a woman, who in her younger days had been sensitive and artistic. Later on she let herself become devitalised by an accumulation of administrative business. At last she went into a retreat, where her spiritual guide gave her one piece of advice, 'Go home and write poetry and try to learn how to write faster.' He was perceptive and he was right. She discovered that when she did not work such very long hours, she could work faster and then had time enough to preserve her vivacity and gifts. The more we grow into Jesus, the more likely our gifts are to blossom.

Fourthly, I am impressed that Jesus had the ability to *live freely and spontaneously, yet to respect authority*. And this is so important for us if we are to grow to maturity; though I see its difficulty wherever I travel, and not only among young people.

Jesus was always doing spontaneous unexpected things; how, to take one example, he welcomed with unprecedented understanding and forgiveness the prostitute, who wept at his feet in the stiff, censorious household of Simon the Pharisee (Luke 7.36-50). Yet all the time he was living in a heavily authoritarian society, both politically and religiously.

His country was *politically* under the Romans, who, as Tacitus himself said, made a desert and called it a peace. Jesus had sympathy with political protest, I presume, as one of his disciples came from the Zealots, a militant liberation group. And, although individual freedom is a corollary of Jesus' teaching, we can find no political policy on his lips. When the people wished to make him king, he slipped away from them (John 6.15). Nor did he respond to the political enthusiasm of the crowds, when he rode on an ass into Jerusalem on Palm Sunday. He also refused to involve himself in a dispute on Roman taxation (Mark 12.13-17). Later on Paul took a similar line to his master. Probably both saw that radical social and political change was not 'on the cards' for the then tiny handful of Christians.

I quite understand how today many Christians take a different line in South America and other parts of the world. *Autres temps, autres moeurs*. In each different situation we need to discover what to attempt and when. We need wisdom and discernment, as well as determination and energy. And we can learn much from works of liberation theology, like the Jesuit Jon Sobrino's *Christology at the Crossroads* and the Franciscan Leonardo Boff's *Jesus Christ Liberator*; they show that to Jesus liberation was not for the individual only, but for humanity through the coming of God's kingdom. I myself would agree with Hans Küng: 'Jesus did not demand and still less did he set in motion a politico-social revolution. What he did set going was decidedly a revolution emerging from man's innermost and secret nature, from the heart of man, a radical change in man's thinking and a conversion, a turning away from all forms of selfishness towards God and his own fellow men.' This inner, basic change is like water, seeping into a crevice in the rocks; then it freezes and cracks them apart.

It is clear that Jesus—and Paul after him—was much more outspoken against *legalistic religious authorities*. Although a political title 'The King of the Jews' was fixed on Jesus' cross on Good Friday, it was the Jewish religious authorities who were responsible for his execution. Jesus was loyal, but *critically loyal*, to the Jewish religious practice based on the Mosaic Law. He joined regularly in synagogue and temple worship. He was orthodox enough to be given the title 'Rabbi'. But clearly he set aside 'extras', added by the lawyers and Pharisees, like ceremonial washings before meals. He frequently healed the sick on the sabbath; because for him these deeds of love were more important than the strict rest from work demanded by the letter of the Law itself. 'The sabbath was made for man', Jesus declared, 'not man for the sabbath.' Jesus taught that the sabbath command was intended to promote man's true good, and not to be a narrow strait-jacket in which he had to be confined. And as Jesus' friends we have to work out what the basic principle involves for the whole of our lives.

This issue came to a head, when the lawyers and Pharisees brought to him a woman caught in the act of adultery. They pestered him to join with them in stoning the woman to death as the Mosaic Law enacted. To them she was not a woman needing to be understood; she was only a test-case. Jesus read her heart and theirs and said, 'The one of you who is without sin, let him throw the first stone at her.' Shamefaced they slunk away one by one. Then Jesus looked at the woman and asked, 'Has no one condemned you?' She answered, 'No one, Lord.' 'Neither do I condemn you', Jesus said. 'Go and do not sin again.' Jesus was—and is—discerning, forgiving, but not condoning (John 8.2-11). As we keep Jesus before our eyes with his sensitivity, love and wisdom, we shall progressively discover how to find the balance between spontaneity and authority for us in our world, a world so inevitably different from his Galilee and Jerusalem.

>For the love of God is broader
>Than the measures of man's mind.

For Jesus came, as we shall soon see, to set us free 'to learn' in the memorable words of Daniel Day Williams 'the art of loving, which is man's high destiny.'

Fifthly, Jesus has also the secret I see of how to hold in a similar balance *personal integrity* and the art of *living together*. There are few things which so much prevent our growing into our true selves as passive, or even resentful, acquiescence in norms expected of us by the group in which we live.

Jesus is clear about the irreplaceable value of everyone's individuality. He tells of the woman who turned the whole house upside down to find the one missing coin (Luke 15.6-10). Not only does Jesus teach this, he lives it. In his love he goes out to all sorts of individuals—even the disreputable and unconventional—to meet them where they are and to encourage them to grow to their full possibilities.

Yet with all his understanding of each individual, he

shows them that it is only within the companionship of others that they can grow to become their true selves. So he calls his apostles, diverse as they are, to grow into their responsibilities by living together with him and with one another. They have their difficulties. They rub each other up the wrong way, they envy one another, and some manoeuvre for personal prominence. 'Grant us the right to sit in state with you,' two of them ask, 'one at your right and the other on your left' (Mark 10.37). But he holds them all together; and it is through resolving their tensions that they grow to their full stature and are trained to carry out their responsibilities. Doubtless it is through living with Jesus himself that they learn step by step to live in his Spirit.

Sixthly, Jesus has the gift of overcoming an even greater hindrance to our true development, that is, our being turned in upon ourselves through fear and *apprehensiveness*. Sometimes we are too afraid to strike out on our own or too apprehensive to come to a firm decision; this may be a temperamental weakness, but it does sap our power of initiative. We can for our encouragement remember that Jesus himself experienced this difficulty. He felt this fear—and yet walked through it. The people at Nazareth, who had known him all his life, were envious and infuriated at his teaching, but he was not intimidated. 'They leapt up,' we read, 'threw him out of the town, and took him to the brow of the hill on which it was built, meaning to hurl him over the edge. But he walked straight through them all, and went away' (Luke 4.29-30). Jesus also knows how well-meaning friends can sometimes try to strike fear into our hearts. When his opponents were massing against him in Judaea and Jerusalem, his disciples tried to dissuade him from going there. 'Rabbi,' they said, 'it is not long since the Jews there were wanting to stone you. Are you going there again?' (John 11.8). Yet undeterred he went.

But courage did not come easily to Jesus, and he admitted this to his friends. When in Gethsemane he saw a terrible death only a hand's-breadth away, he begged the help of their prayers: 'My heart is ready to break with grief; stop here, and stay awake.' (Mark 14.34). Prayer itself that night in Gethsemane was a hard struggle even for Jesus himself. But in the end he could get up from his prayer with courage renewed. 'Enough! The hour has come. The Son of man is betrayed to sinful men', he said. 'Up, let us go forward! My betrayer is upon us' (Mark 14.41-42). So he then went forward with love-inspired courage to his sufferings, which culminated in the agony of his crucifixion; and at the end he could even in his intense pain declare with a deep confidence, 'It is accomplished.' (John 19.30). His life-task was completed. And so in some mysterious way he had set in motion new liberating powers of love for us all.

Jesus knew his followers would have love and joy, but also unavoidable sufferings. 'If they have persecuted me, they will also persecute you.' So hardships and frustrations should never take us by surprise. The earliest Christians were warned of cataclysmic events to come. 'Nation will make war upon nation, kingdom upon kingdom; there will be famines and earthquakes in many places.' (Matt. 24.7). The people of the first century AD felt that their future was at the mercy of implacable, astrological cosmic powers, 'principalities and powers, and world rulers of this present darkness' (Col. 1.13, 16; 2.15; Eph. 6.12). Gilbert Murray, a great authority on the Graeco-Roman world, said that it suffered from 'a loss of nerve'—and no wonder.

We cannot accept literally the astrological beliefs of the first century. But we are conscious of forces of evil abroad in our world too. How else can we explain the sadistic cruelty inflicted on the Jews in Germany before and during the last war? How else can we explain the sheer inhumanity of other régimes in our own times? And we may live to see economic collapse or social disintegration or even some terrible escalating war, perhaps a major atomic war, triggered off maybe by some irresponsible person. Fear is understandable. But we must try never to retreat faint-heartedly, paralysed, from considered action. Paul says that it is because our conflict is not merely against human foes but these cosmic powers, that we must 'find our strength in the Lord and in the power of his might' (Eph. 6.10). So our eyes are drawn back again to the Lord Jesus.

Behind these inner qualities of Jesus, beneath all his wisdom, discernment and courage, is his praying. He is what he is, because he so prays and loves. We all know that obstacles get in the way of our growing, and we will next see how Jesus helps us to be set free from them. But let us now reflect prayerfully on how far we have managed to come already in this discovery of our true selves.

'A life not reflected on is not a truly human life.'
'Lo, I am with you always', says the Lord.
Help us, Lord, to be still—to be still and reflect.
In Jesus we see what God is really like.
And in Jesus we see what being really human is like.
Real humanness means growing into our true relationship with God,
and our true relationship with one another.
How can I grow into outgoing love,
how can I make lasting friendships,
how can I discover my gifts,
how can I be spontaneous without forgetting the
wisdom of others,
how can I be myself and yet live with others,
how can I face the future with courage?
Lord, show me how really to pray.

4   THE CROSS AND LIBERATION

'What's wrong with the world?' was the topic between the two world wars of a long correspondence in the London *Times*. Those were the years of a worldwide slump, of the rise of Fascists and Nazis and of the purge in Stalin's Russia. One of the most perceptive of these letters was the shortest; it came from the well-known author, Mr Chesterton, and it read: 'Dear Sir, *I* am. Yours sincerely, G. K. Chesterton.'

It was not a complete answer, but it was an integral part of any real answer. And Christians believe that the Cross brings liberation from sin and other evils. 'But how can a death two thousand years ago', people ask, 'liberate us from evil today?' This profound question has challenged Christian thinkers down the centuries. I can give only the beginning of an answer, which I would like you to reflect on further. But we cannot expect to understand the death of Jesus until we first begin to understand his life. For it is not his dying in itself that can set us free, but his ever-constant loving, which inspired him to lay down his life for us.

HIS DECISION TO LOVE

Jesus decided to love—and to do nothing else. This is how he began his life-work. This choice is what lies behind the temptations at the start of his ministry. He was then deciding that love itself should be the sole motivation for all his life.

What he lived, he taught. Someone once asked him what life was all about and what really mattered in it. He replied, 'What matters most is that we love God with the whole of our personalities and so love our neighbours as much as we love ourselves'. 'Everything else', he added, 'is subsidiary to this and depends on it.'

Jesus persisted in this love-inspired living through all his experiences, great and small, congenial and uncongenial, right the way through. 'Having loved his own that were in the world, he loved them to the end' (John 13.1). We see this in the way he teaches, in the way he heals, and in the way he challenges others.

HIS LIFE-WORK OF LOVE

As Jesus teaches, he looks into the eyes of those who are before him, and his heart is aware of their problems. He sees their deepest need is love; and he knows how through lack of love they so easily belittle themselves and so become discouraged and devitalised. So he speaks to them of God their Father who in his love for them runs down the road to greet and embrace them *before* they reach home. Jesus' words go echoing down the centuries and speak directly to us today. His teaching is his loving.

We watch how he heals. The sick are brought to him; as his eyes rest upon them, he not only notices their symptoms, but also sees the wounds inflicted by hard experiences in their hearts. Love brings them inward and outer healing. 'Your sins are forgiven', he says; 'rise up and walk.' It is his love that will give to us the particular kind of healing we need, so that we can then discover our true selves.

Then we notice that Jesus challenges people—though not in any superior olympian way—but because he loves them and wants them to think and to grow. We might have thought that his consistent and thoroughgoing love would have made him popular. Quite the contrary. Many of the lawyers and Pharisees opposed him. Over the years they had built around themselves a hard shell, as it were, of legal decisions. Inside this shell they were shrivelling up and losing their human warmth. They thought that any problem, however intricate and personal, could be answered out of a legal book if the book were large enough and detailed enough. We have seen

45

how sharply this issue was raised when the Pharisees brought to Jesus a woman taken in adultery. Jesus knew that every situation and every person must be approached with fresh understanding and love; and that books can give no more than useful, general guidelines.

Jesus saw that he could not bring to these men God's forgiveness and love and so restore them to real humanness, unless he could first break through this hard shell. So with strong words Jesus challenged them—and through them he challenges those with legalistic minds all down the centuries. He called them whited sepulchres. He was speaking the truth in love. And Jesus' love like all real love is not weak.

LOVE AND THE WRATH OF GOD

So we see love, even in Jesus' attitude to the Pharisees. But you may be asking yourself, 'And what about the other side, the "wrath" of God?' Nowhere in the New Testament is the verb 'to be angry' used of God, although similar personal verbs, like 'to hate' and 'to have compassion', are applied to him. And when the Old Testament says that God is angry, then we need to read the Old, as Augustine said, in the light of the New and not the other way round. The New Testament uses the corresponding noun 'anger' or 'wrath' normally only in an impersonal way as 'the anger' or 'the wrath'; it speaks of wrath as the 'wrath of God' only three times (Rom. 1.18; Eph. 5.6; Col. 3.6). What does all this add up to? I think it is that 'the wrath' is nearly always an impersonal term like 'the storm' or 'the tempest'. I believe *the* wrath is one aspect of God's powerful love. For the New Testament says that God *is* love itself; not that love is one of God's attributes, perhaps the most prominent, and wrath another, different attribute. So, as far as I can see, the wrath is like an autumn storm which strips the trees of their leaves. They are ultimately better for the storm, because only when the old leaves and dead wood are shaken off will the trees put forth the vitality and fresh beauty of spring. It is because God loves us and

46

wishes to see in us new vitality and beauty, that his love manifests itself in the autumn gale of his wrath to blow off the old leaves, which have served their purpose, and all else that is second-rate and past its best.

LOVE AND LIBERATION

Love or no love, the lawyers and Pharisees—strict, religious, upright men though they were—could not stand these gale-like challenges of Jesus. They hated him for undermining their elaborate system. They plotted to get rid of him. When Jesus went to Jerusalem for the last time, he was still resolved to meet everyone and face every situation with this consistent, open-eyed love. He would not even at the risk of his life seek a compromise of half-love-half-law. He said he had come 'to serve not to be served'; to love and so 'to give his life a ransom for many' (Mark 10.45).

In our violent world we talk about ransoming hostages; in Jesus' world they talked about ransoming slaves. In his days men and women stood as slaves, sometimes manacled, in the market-place. They could not break free until some benefactor paid down their ransom-price. The fetters were then snapped; and they were free. Jesus by his consistent loving, right until his last breath, saw himself becoming our liberator; he was setting in action a new power of liberating love which could progressively set us free; but free from what?— from sin, which perhaps needs some re-defining; and also from temperamental and similar defects; from ingrained excessive egoism; and from the power of cosmic evil. From these things we need to be set free in order to love and, in loving, to become our true selves.

Jesus and the New Testament Christians think of liberation as liberation from sin through forgiveness. Jesus tells us that he has come 'to call sinners to repentance'. In his final words to his disciples he declares that 'repentance bringing forgiveness of sins is to be proclaimed to all nations'. We read in the first letter of Peter: 'Christ died for our sins, once for all, the righteous for the unrighteous, that he might bring us to God'. But Christians in the past have often used the word 'sin' in a narrow, external, legalistic sort of way. They have taken over, without enough new reflection, catalogues of external sins from the Old Testament. They have also found it easier and quicker to evaluate other people by their external actions than by taking the trouble to try to see what is really 'going on inside them'. Jesus himself followed this second and deeper way; for example, he concerned himself not only with violence and murder, but even more with hearts empty of real love, because this is the source from which all cruel words and acts spring (Matt. 5.21-22).

Sin is lack of love—it is not responding with our love to God's love; it is not loving, not being truly concerned for our neighbours; and it is not loving ourselves in the sense of not having a true appreciation and care of ourselves. St John of the Cross wrote perceptively: 'At eventide we shall be examined about love.'

Secondly, we need to be set free also from temperamental and similar defects, for our personalities are shaped by our inner defects as much as by our talents. These defects are different from sins, which are, strictly speaking, deliberate and conscious. To make this distinction clear, let us reflect for a moment why, on occasions, we do not go out in love to make contact with others in the way Jesus did. It is sometimes because we choose arrogantly and so sinfully not to do so. But at other times it is only because our shyness and other temperamental defects hold us back. These defects, which may be partly the result of our upbringing, are not sins; yet they prevent us really helping other people.

Most of us, however, can do something towards overcoming these temperamental handicaps. Some of us may seek skilled counselling. And all of us need love, for it is love, divine and human, which above all heals us from these defects. We will consider this further when we look at the transforming power of the Spirit.

But perhaps these particular sins and defects have rooted themselves in our lives, because we have taken for our ideal not the warm, rich humanness of Jesus, but some cooler, more stoical character. We may even have cultivated an indifference to others because we have regarded them as boring, ungifted people, and we've said we are 'too busy' to have time for them.

Indifference to people, William Temple used to say, was the worst possible way to treat anyone. Indifference, he explained, is worse than anger, because anger at least acknowledges the other person's existence, while indifference just tries to write him off. Further, anger and indignation are integral strands of our human nature as much as sympathy and tenderness, or as our sense of beauty and wonder. They all need to be woven together into our personalities; and it is love that does the weaving. Indignation and anger we see in the character of Jesus himself, as whip in hand he drives the profiteers out of the temple. These basic energies of his are directed by love—love for God, who desires worshippers to come to him in spirit and in truth; and love for these people in the temple, who were being taken advantage of; and love for the traders, because love for them demands that their greed for money should be restrained. Jesus lived and died to bring to us all this liberating love.

Thirdly, we need to be liberated from that ingrained excessive egoism, which is sometimes called the 'fallenness' of our human nature. There is of course a right type of egoism, a right kind of appreciation and cultivation of ourselves, which incidentally involves making adequate time for reflection and prayer. But there is also widespread excessive egoism, an undue preoccupation with ourselves, our ambitions, our security. So we catch ourselves almost automatically thinking at the time of a crisis, at the time of a strike, at almost any time: 'How will this affect *me*?'—not 'How will it affect the underprivileged, or my colleagues, or the country as a whole or the world?' We have deep within us this bias towards an excessive self-concern. We are like bowls in the English game of bowling; we have a bias, we don't run straight, we swerve towards our own interests. However it has arisen, this 'fallenness' of our human nature is one of our chief obstacles in discovering who we are and what we are capable of becoming. We need liberation from this bias.

Unfortunately this bias is self-propagating; for the more we yield to it, the stronger it grows; and the stronger it grows in us, the stronger our neighbours normally let it grow in themselves in sheer self-defence. Humanity is entangled in this web of excessive egoism. Today, more than ever in the past, we can as men and women glimpse our immense human potential for good; and yet seldom have we seen so clearly the misery of our serious predicament—loneliness and frustration, corruption and violence, economic hazards and the threat of war.

Yet Jesus has come into this confused situation. He lived a life of unceasing love, which reached its culmination on the cross. By doing so he has set in motion this new dynamic of love and of hope. It is because Jesus has in this way given to all humanity a fresh beginning, that Paul has called Jesus the new Adam, the new start.

This brings us to the fourth aspect of our liberation, our being set free from the power of cosmic evil; for humanity, entangled in this pervasive, excessive egoism, is humanity endangered by these forces of evil.

The earliest evangelists show Jesus, not only drawing men and women nearer to God and nearer to one another through forgiveness and love, but also defeating the powers of evil. We have seen already how strong a sense of these cosmic powers of evil the first Christians had. Paul also depicts Jesus' victory over evil in even more vivid, though symbolical, language. In his letter to the Colossians, for instance, he writes in a baffling sentence that the power of Jesus' love, manifested most clearly on the cross, was so great that it disarmed these cosmic powers and led them as captives in his triumphal procession (Col. 2.15).

This same conviction very probably lies behind Jesus' dying words in John's gospel, 'It is accomplished.' These words are not a sigh of relief at the ending of his pain; they are rather a cry of victory. His life-task of love is completed, and the forces of evil are broken. On the cross Jesus had reached the climax of his life of unswerving love and there the decisive battle over evil had been won. The rest of our campaign against evil is like a gigantic mopping-up operation. For the enemy's morale is beginning to crack up, and the evil which we still fight is already on the run, a more than half-defeated foe, yet putting up, as we know, some tough rearguard actions. The final victory is certain, though we do not know whether we shall see it in history or beyond human history. This is the conviction that has given to countless Christians courage, joy and resilience in all their combat with evil. 'In the world you will have trouble. But courage! The victory is mine; I have conquered the world' (John 16.33). There is all this—and much more—for us to reflect and meditate on in the great liberation which Jesus in his immense, unalterable love offers to us.

LOVE AND THE WAY OF THE CROSS

Jesus was convinced that his love was going to bring us liberation. This gave him the courage to take the road to the cross. This is what kept him going. How much he could at that time see of the immense fanning out of this liberation, we cannot know. But we must not measure his knowledge, even while on earth, by our own. Great men and women of prayer—Mother Julian of Norwich, Teresa of Lisieux, Teilhard de Chardin—could see the repercussions of love and prayer much further that we can, to say nothing of Jesus himself.

So we watch him through the closing hours of his life of unflagging love. In that Jerusalem upper room at the last supper, the first eucharist, he gives himself, without any reservation, in love to the Father and to us; he takes the chalice into his hands and says, 'This is my blood, the blood of the covenant, shed for many for the forgiveness of sins'. He consecrates himself afresh, he re-affirms his determination to go on courageously loving to the very end and so in a mysterious way to bring us this forgiveness and liberation.

From the warmth and light of that upper room he goes out into the coldness of the night to pray in the blackness of the garden of Gethsemane. He has to struggle, as sometimes we do, to keep himself aligned to God's calling and purpose for him. He wins through, as we have seen, to meet without flinching his betrayer and his arrest.

This love-inspired courage now sustains him through his trials before the high priest and before Pilate, through being beaten up, through dragging his massive cross along the narrow, winding alleyways of Jerusalem. But even now his thoughts are not for himself and his own pain, but still for others and for their future. So he speaks to the women of Jerusalem who wept in pity for him: 'Daughters of Jerusalem, do not weep for me; no, weep for yourselves and your children', as he foresees the horrors that were to come on their city. And a little later in his hour of extreme pain as the men are actually fixing him on his cross, he prays for their forgiveness and tries to excuse their cruelty.

As we stay with him during those long, slow hours on the cross, we are drawn to this love-impelled man, one who through suffering has grown to be his true self. But not only do we see in him real humanness, we see also the divine love, God's love at its uttermost, for he who sees Jesus sees God. For God is no distant creator, no remote lawgiver. He is one who is very close to us in unceasing love, sharing our worries, our frustrations and our sufferings.

If we wish to know what our sin does to God and means to God, we see it in Jesus crucified. If we would understand how God regards us as we go on sinning and not responding to his love, we see this in Jesus during his passion. Surely we cannot go on in our cold ways, in our being indifferent to others, when we grasp that by doing this we are wounding the heart of the One who loved us so deeply that he prayed even for those who were crucifying him: 'Father, forgive them; they do not know what they are doing.' None of us can remain insensitive and unloving, *if* we become aware that we are really loved in this way. I began to be more conscious of this love at that small Wisconsin lake, but I know I have very much more to find out about this truth that 'God was in Christ reconciling the world to himself', and to make it really part of myself.

Ever since Jesus died on Good Friday and was raised to life on Easter day, he has actually been bringing this power of liberating love into the lives of countless people. We can see it in history and in our own observation. We watch men and women being progressively set free from a lack of real love, from their weaknesses, self-centredness, fears and anxieties. Many of them were much like ourselves; some, much more handicapped. The Acts of the Apostles and Paul's letters show us that. Corinth was an eastern seaport, full of idolatry, roguery, licentiousness, so much so that the Greeks had a special word for living a dissolute life: it was 'to corinthianise'. But Paul could write to the Christians there: 'You were like that, but now you have been liberated, cleansed. You now belong to the Lord, you have been put into a true relation with God.'

And so it has gone on down to our own times. A young man used to go into churches in Paris and pray, 'My God, if you are God, show yourself to me.' Both of his parents had died before he was six, and he had been spoilt by his grandfather. He lost his faith. He was an idle spendthrift; he finished eighty-seventh in a class of eighty-seven at a military academy. This Charles de Foucauld was a reckless young officer. Sent to Algeria, he pretended his mistress was his wife and resigned his commission in a row with his colonel. He threw up his girl and went off in disguise and alone to explore Morocco, then a completely closed country. He was impressed by the Moslem men at prayer. Then back in Paris he one day went into the Church of St Augustine near the Opéra and said to a priest: 'Father, I've lost my faith; I want instruction.' This discerning guide, Abbé Huvelin, replied, 'It is not instruction you need but absolution.' He confessed. His clouds of doubt dispersed, and God became a reality to him.

Soon he was a Trappist and then a hermit among the illiterate Tuaregs around Tamanrasset in the Sahara. He compiled the first Tuareg grammar and dictionary, wrote down for them their proverbs and love-songs and translated the gospels. In his love he identified himself with them. He even wrote to Marie, his cousin in Paris, to send him some black hair-dye to conceal the greying hair of the Tuareg women. The liberating love of Jesus led him to the heart of everyone; so they said of him.

He was shot dead during the first world war by some anti-French tribesmen. His life looked a failure, like a grain of wheat falling into the ground to die. But his loving, his praying and his writings have borne a rich harvest. He is the man who has inspired the Little Brothers and Sisters of Jesus. I have met them all over the world, the freshest and most joyful community I know. His love has touched thousands within and outside almost all the Churches. He has become what he prayed that he might be, 'le frère universel', the brother open to all. Christ is indeed liberator.

> Lord, you are with me now and always.
> Help me to meditate on your unswerving love
>   in how you taught;
>   how you healed;
>   how you challenged others;
>   and in how you went to Jerusalem to die for us
>   to liberate us
>   to love
>   in the way you loved.

5 A RESPONSE OF LOVE

A husband gave his wife a wedding anniversary present, an expensive one, partly to compensate for his recent neglect of her through his being so engrossed in his job. 'Thank you more than I can say', she said with tears in her eyes. 'But what I really want is you and your love.'

All that God in his love has done for us will make no practical difference to us, unless we respond personally. And the only real response to love is love. At first it may not so much be love, as wanting to love—yet that in itself is the beginning of love. No other response, even if well organised, will get us anywhere. I've seen that only too often. 'God asks not for heroes but for lovers', Rowan Williams rightly says, 'not for moral athletes but for men and women who are aware of their need.' And this response of love, Jesus himself explains, will express itself in two linked up ways. 'The time has come; the kingdom of God is at your doors', he says, 'repent and believe'.

CONFIDENCE AND REPENTANCE

In the New Testament 'to believe' is not to accept a statement, but to put your confidence in a person—in God who actually comes (what good news this is!) to us in Jesus. Our initial confidence in God may be as small as a grain of mustard seed, but it will grow if we really want it to. When we trust as far as we can, we often find ourselves able to trust at least a little further. To come to God with whatever confidence we can is the first step towards our being liberated to love.

But besides trusting we have to find out how to *repent*. This doesn't mean being miserable or belittling ourselves. The Greek word for it in the gospels, *metanoia*, means a turning round of the mind. This is the inner

Copernican revolution, which William Temple used to say was the fundamental need of all of us. You see what he means. Before the time of Copernicus we used to think that the earth was the focus of the universe and that the sun and moon wheeled round us. But then Copernicus showed that the sun is the focus and we move round the sun on our proper orbit. We all need the corresponding change. The focus of our lives needs to be steadily shifted from self to God. This process is *metanoia*, and it is our maturing into our true selves. This change is not easy because of that egoistical bias in our nature. But all the time God's love for us, which attracts us to himself as a magnet attracts steel, is trying to bring about this change of focus. As we love him in return we collaborate with him in our inner Copernican revolution.

It really starts with our forgiveness and the absolution of our sins. Unless we let him begin here, God cannot effectively liberate us also from our temperamental defects, from our ingrained excessive egoism and from our fear of cosmic powers of evil. So *metanoia* is the key to this liberation we all at heart desire. And how then do we in practice begin it? Let me say, God doesn't want us to be preoccupied with self-introspection. I'm not interested in sin, but in God and his love.

DAILY FORGIVENESS

The way we deepen our human relationships will I think show us how to find our way. As a priest I have often tried to help couples prepare themselves for marriage. For one thing in particular several of them have come back and thanked me. I had suggested that before the end of each day they should try to make up any differences they might have had. I know it's not easy, it requires sensitivity, love and sometimes courage. But if there is something we can't talk over together and, if necessary, forgive, then there is a kind of small blockage between us. And, if these blockages aren't cleared up each day, they can pile up into a real barrier. 'We can't

56

talk about that sort of thing', one or other may say. Then they may be living together but they are not really together.

Many of us know that this is true also in our relationship with God. We want nothing to come between us. So we know we need day by day to come to him with love and confidence and speak to him about our failings and then be sure we are forgiven.

In our human relationships sometimes we half sense that something is wrong; and we know that things can't be right again, until we have found the appropriate moment to talk them over together. With God it is in some ways different. He knows our failings without our telling him. But to tell him is such a relief to us. It is bottled-up faults that cause us worry and trouble. And we have discovered how vital it is to us to be able to share our shortcomings and troubles with him. It needn't be over-solemn or long-drawn-out. We find that this way of being open with him is an essential part of our growing closer to him in love.

With me it goes like this. I sit down quietly each evening—not last thing at night, if I can help it, as I am rather tired then. I know God is near me and very understanding, and I remember his love for me disclosed so clearly in Jesus. Then I look back over my day. There is always plenty to thank him for. But I feel I must also speak to him about my faults, my failures in love to him and to others. I say them out—a piece of work for others which I didn't put my best into; or saying 'I haven't time' to someone who needed a few minutes that I could have found; or making no effort to appreciate a particular person, very different from Frère Roger's way of meeting others. I don't let myself be vague in this confessing to God. That helps me also to see just where I need his strength.

And then, it is like being with a close friend. I don't let myself be in a hurry. I remain quiet, still, receptive, so as really to be aware of God's forgiveness. Each of us needs to find how best to let this forgiveness sink in. Praying, like loving, isn't just thinking. Praying, again like loving, involves our bodies too. What would love be like without embraces? So in the quietness which follows my saying out my faults, personally I make the sign of the cross with my hand, remembering that for my forgiveness the Lord came down into the world, stretched out his arms in love upon the cross and was raised to life and love again. And often I then say peacefully and gratefully:

He loved and did nothing else;
He died that we might be forgiven;
He was raised to life to put us right with God.

I use this small confession as part of my preparation for going the next day to Holy Communion. If you can go to Holy Communion only on Sundays and great festivals, you could make your review slightly longer, covering the time since your last communion. Then when in church we say the general confession of sins with the rest of the congregation, we can bear in mind what we actually need to have forgiven. We can also tell God where we think we particularly need his strength through this sacrament.

WORDS OF ABSOLUTION

Years ago in a London church where I was giving a course, I had been speaking about confessing our faults. I happened to be in the church the next morning when quite an old man, not particularly well educated or at all religious, came up to me. I thought my address the evening before had annoyed him. But not at all. We talked things over together. He thought about it for a time. Then he hobbled his way up the church to where I was sitting, and he confessed all he could remember of his life in fairly blunt language. I assured him of God's forgiveness. I have never seen an old man's face change as his did. He had received the peace that passes all understanding.

Only God can forgive, but we are so made that we often need a human voice to assure us of his forgiveness. The prostitute who came to Jesus at a feast in the Pharisee's house knew in her heart that God would certainly forgive her, because God is always ready to forgive us and nothing is beyond being forgiven. But she knew she needed to hear the words, 'Thy sins are forgiven, go in peace.' It's the same in friendship and love. Because we are human, we know that, when we have had some misunderstanding, it is just not enough to feel in a vague, general way that it is 'all over and done with'. We need to hear words that will heal the relationship. 'I understand, I forgive. Let us start together afresh.' Real peace with God and the joy and vitality of new life come to many of us only *after* we have heard Jesus' words through human lips. I know the day and place when I first heard them. I was a student then. It was a difficult first confession. But I remember, as if it were yesterday, the peace and encouragement that then came to me.

If some people hesitate to ask for the assurance of God's forgiveness in this way, it is quite understandable; and I would always wish them to come to their own open-eyed decision about it. They may be shy and rather reserved by nature. We can't and mustn't try to change our temperaments overnight. And like many new experiences this needs courage initially. Yet this same shyness, as we have seen, may be a root-cause of our lack of outgoing love to others; and so confession itself may help us to overcome it as well as to make us sure of our forgiveness.

The gift of receiving forgiveness in this way may sometimes have been misused. So have other gifts—even friendship and marriage itself. And the fact that others have misused this gift of confession need not delay our wise use of it.

In different Churches, people have in various ways come to their ministers to receive through them the assurance of God's forgiveness. This has been clearly so in the Eastern Orthodox Churches, in the Roman Catholic Church, and to a lesser extent in the Anglican and other Churches. The Lutheran, Dietrich Bonhoeffer, has written very understandingly about it in his book, *Life Together*; and so has Max Thurian, of the

Reformed Church among the Taizé brothers, in his book, *Confession*. 'Confession is good for you' is a layman's catch-phrase in a world where people speak so freely to their psychiatrists. We may not need to go to confession very frequently; and certainly we must not become spiritual hypochondriacs, always going round with spiritual thermometers in our mouths!

So let us look practically and positively at why many people go to a priest or minister to receive God's forgiveness—in fact probably many more do so than we think; and then consider other workaday aspects of it. We have, I think, four motives. The first is the twofold desire both to express our sorrow as truly and deeply as we can for our repeated faults which have grieved God, wounded his love and harmed those whom we should have loved and helped; and also to receive as effectively as possible the forgiveness and liberating love for which Jesus came, lived, died and rose again to bring us.

Secondly we feel, and rightly feel, that if in this kind of confession we can bring ourselves to 'put all our cards on the table', we shall be able to receive better and more informed advice to overcome our faults and failings. In particular people often feel—and it is true—that this is one of the most effective methods of gradually dispelling that grey sense of discouragement that so easily settles down on our life of prayer and of human relationships.

Thirdly, we come to see more clearly how our sins are related to those inner defects which have largely come from our upbringing, education and from past unhappy experience of life. For as we have seen, our personalities are fashioned by these defects as much as by our gifts. We also see more precisely how our way of praying and living is mis-shaped by our egoistical bias and by our fears of powers of evil beyond ourselves.

Fourthly, when we feel that it is time that we should live more consistently a life of Christian praying, loving and serving, we realise we require the discipline of receiving regularly from time to time the skilled advice and encouragement we are sure to need. We can't be disciples without a freely accepted, appropriate discipline.

And we need a guide to keep in review not only the opportunities and potentialities of our lives, but also the significant dark corners, which most of us are so apt to hide, even from ourselves.

If we are going to do our best in some study, art or sport, we know we must find a personal tutor, teacher or coach. So if we want to grow in prayer and love, we must look, I think, for an experienced guide—or in a phrase of Alexander Pope, 'a guide, philosopher and friend'; and then we should arrange a preliminary talk with him. John Calvin, the great reformer, said that the pastor, on account of his vocation and training, might be our obvious choice. We must find out if he is sufficiently 'on our beam', so that we can speak freely about ourselves and our experiences. We often live too close to ourselves to see ourselves as we are. And it is part of a priest's ministry to help us to be objective. He will of course never betray a confidence. We can be sure of that.

Francis de Sales at the beginning of his guide-book to Christian living and praying wrote: 'Seek out some good man to guide and conduct you; this is the admonition of admonitions.' We see also from Charles de Foucauld's letters how the Abbé Huvelin helped him to experience the liberating power of God's love not only in his first confession but throughout his life-journey.

In our desire to be drawn progressively nearer to God and so to love and serve others better, many Christians find it is a great help to make a review of their lives perhaps before Christmas and Easter and during a retreat in the summer. Let me tell you a way I find useful for this longer kind of review. I take pen and paper; that helps me to be clearer and more practical. Then I am silent for a few minutes; I realise that God is with me now and always, and I remind myself I am not concerned primarily to examine my life but to deepen my relationship of love with the Lord. I am not expected to imitate the external details of his life—that would be impossible, as we have seen. But the inner strands of my character need to be made more like his; this is essential if we really are to be closer to him and to one another. All the time I need to remember how with the liberating power of his love he himself is trying to make this inner change within me.

So I ask him to help me by his Spirit to see where in my ordinary life I am helping him to do this or hindering him. Then I know that with the help of my guide I shall see more clearly where my basic weaknesses are and where my prayer, service and love need to be reinvigorated.

After my preparation I arrange to see my guide and confessor. This is normally but not necessarily in church. I know he won't be shocked by anything I may say. This is his job, like the doctor in the surgery. No one need ever say, 'After this confession I shall never be able to face him again.' I have never found any embarrassment of that kind. The priest who heard my first confession remained one of my closest friends. Nor should we ever say, 'It's no good my confessing that; I might do it again.' Of course we might; but it is better to go to confession and apologise, even if we slip again, than to be too proud to apologise at all.

Jesus himself intended, I think, that his ministers should help others in this way. Jesus understood our human nature so deeply; he himself gave so many this inner certainty of God's complete forgiveness; and he knew that, after he would be visibly no longer in this world, men and women would still have this same need. So on the first Easter evening he came to his disciples and authorised them through the help of his Holy Spirit to continue what he had been doing himself. 'Receive the Holy Spirit', he said; 'If you forgive any man's sins, they are forgiven; if you pronounce them unforgiven, unforgiven they remain.' It looks to me that he expected people one by one to admit their sins to the apostles. And I should think that the apostles would normally say, 'Your sins are forgiven; go in peace.' Only if there was obvious insincerity would an apostle have to say, 'No, I cannot at present assure you of God's forgiveness.'

We know how important gurus are to men and women of other faiths. In the Christian tradition we see the beginning of this art of personal guidance in the New Testament. Philemon, Timothy and Titus received letters of direction. We have also the advice in the letter of James: 'Confess your sins one to another, and pray for one another, and then you will be healed' (Jas. 5.16). For, as Jesus showed us, we need not only the healing of our bodies but an inner healing from wounds that life has inflicted on us, and both may depend on the removal of unhealthy guilt.

Perhaps confession and 'professional' guidance is not the precise way for everyone. But we all need to face the facts about ourselves, to be no longer discouraged by failures, to live closer to Christ. We don't want to live in a spiritual cloud-cuckoo-land; but rather to bring his love and joy to those round about us, to the world in its need. Forgiveness of the past matters, but that is only half of what matters. The larger half—if we may be so unmathematical—is to know within ourselves both for the present and even more for the future the liberating love of Jesus, our ever-present Risen Lord.

Before we go on to that, perhaps we should pause for reflection and prayer, for we need to be able to say not 'I think God understands my situation and will forgive me' but 'I *know* he has forgiven me.'

Be still, and consider the love and power of the Lord.
Lord, there is much in my past which I cannot understand.
Thank you for what you are now showing me.
In the years to come may you and your love be more real to me,
    and may I understand others better;
    may my prayers and my love help them.
For this to happen I so much need you
    to forgive my sins,
    to handle my defects,

to help me to face my Copernican revolution,
to give me courage,
   so that I do not retire within myself
      in face of the problems and dangers of the
world:
How can I best accept and live in your liberating
love?

6 'YES' TO THE RISEN JESUS

'Too many Christians', a New Testament professor at Glasgow used to say, 'live on the wrong side of Easter.'

They think that to be a Christian means following, as literally as possible, in the footsteps of Jesus. In the world of today they find this a difficult and often discouraging experience. But they go on trying—as they remember how Jesus lived heroically a life of unceasing love, and how he died with arms outstretched on the cross for love of us. So they carry on. They are mistaken, the professor commented; and he added that in the New Testament the fundamental truth about a Christian is not that he follows Jesus and loves him, but that he lives *in* Christ, the Risen Jesus.

This is of first importance for us today. We are not expected to live on our own natural resources, nor to follow Jesus by our own will-power, nor even to respond to him with our own love. We are called to live *in* Christ in the ever-present, living, Risen Jesus, in his own Easter power and joy. For the same divine power that turned Good Friday into Easter day could be energising inside us. Paul tells us that we as Christians should be discovering 'how very great is his power at work in us who believe'; and we should be aware that the 'power working in us is the same mighty strength which God used when he raised Christ from death' (Eph. 1.19-20).

This was Paul's own experience. It was the present, Risen Jesus who met him that day on the road to Damascus—not the Jesus of the past, of Galilee and Jerusalem. Later on in a letter to the Corinthians Paul described how during Eastertide Jesus appeared to the apostles, and then he said explicitly that this same risen Lord 'appeared last of all to me also' (1 Cor. 15.8). So on that ever-memorable day for Paul it was the Risen Jesus who began to set him free from Jewish legalism and to help him—if I may put it this way—'discover his true self'.

We too are invited 'to find our true selves' by encountering the Risen Jesus, by living on the right side of Easter.

This involves intellectual questions about historical evidence. God has given us minds. To exercise our minds is part of our becoming truly human. To use our minds to seek the truth is part of our loving God, not with our emotions only, but with our entire personality.

But did the resurrection really happen? Did the disciples get it right? What really was it? I have myself looked at these questions, long and hard. I've been, as I have told you, an unbeliever. Later as a New Testament lecturer I had to read books that were radical as well as conservative. And more recently since my experience by the Wisconsin lake I've had to probe more deeply than ever, because I can now see how essential it is for me that I should have this inner certitude that Jesus is risen and that we can live in the power of his resurrection. I can only speak for myself. But I am convinced that unless I can live *in* the Risen Christ, I shall never be able to grow into my true self and so be able to do my best to serve my neighbours.

Now, for the resurrection of Christ, as we have seen for the reality of God, there are not the kind of compelling demonstrations that we have in Euclidean geometry. But there are three pointers which invite us to go forward and explore for ourselves. Some people may find one pointer more impressive than the others.

The first pointer is the remarkable change that came over the early Christians after the crucifixion—a change for me inexplicable without Jesus' resurrection. In the night before Good Friday Peter three times denied his Lord. 'I don't know him; I've had nothing to do with him.' And at Jesus' arrest the rest of the disciples fled. Yet within weeks Peter from a flat housetop said to a

Jerusalem crowd, 'You are responsible for the death of one who was innocent.' For this they might have lynched him. But Peter went on and declared, 'God has raised him to life again.' He spoke with such conviction that three thousand that day became Christians. The other apostles, who had fled for their lives, added their witness to Jesus' resurrection. They were now ready to go to prison for their belief in the Risen Lord.

Paul's life is evidence too. He claimed, as we have just seen, that he saw the Risen Jesus on that road to Damascus just as really as the first disciples met him at Easter time. He wrote, 'Am I not an apostle? Did I not see the Lord?' (1 Cor. 9.1). It is this encounter with the Risen Jesus which alone can explain his sudden change from being a violent persecutor of the first Christians into Paul, the outstanding missionary in that Mediterranean world. His life was now completely devoted to the gospel, packed with travelling and writing, with perils and controversies. And his gospel was focussed on the death and resurrection of Jesus. If Jesus had not been raised, Paul wrote, then he and the apostles would 'turn out to be lying witnesses for God' (1 Cor. 15.15).

It was this conviction that God had raised Jesus from death which continued to give the disciples and the first Christians courage to face even martyrdom. It enabled them to face the ferocity of Nero's persecution in Rome. And the same courage has appeared again and again down the centuries until our own days, so producing a movement which indisputably has altered world history.

What happened at Easter generated not only new courage, but also a new love for their Lord and for their neighbours. It impelled the first Christians in Jerusalem to pool their goods as they lived together with an un-heard-of spontaneity and joy. Hundreds of others saw it and were attracted to their Lord. There were of course failures and relapses. But these young Christian communities springing up, often in surprising places around the Mediterranean, brought new courage, joy and love into the world. They were convinced that this new life was theirs only because it came from the Risen Jesus, that they were living, as Paul says, 'in the power of Jesus' resurrection'.

This is our first pointer. It impresses me. But I would like now to add a few words about its relation to your life and mine today. Many of our contemporaries are unlikely to see this pointer, as they have no inclination to read and reflect on the New Testament. But if they could see this courage and love-in-action in some Christian community and in our lives—a kind of love which they do not see much in evidence anywhere else—that might start them inquiring about God and about what he has done for us in the Risen Jesus. They might begin to ask, 'Where does it come from?' We ourselves then would become part of this first pointer to the Risen Lord.

For the second pointer we have to examine the evidence for the empty tomb. Before we do that, I would like us to consider three preliminary matters.

First, we mustn't think of Jesus' resurrection in too naive a way. The gospels make it clear that Jesus' body was not merely resuscitated, re-animated. His friends did not at first recognise him after his resurrection. Jesus was indeed raised, but also transformed and glorified. Of course he was real, not a kind of a ghost, for he had still on his body the marks of the nails. The empty tomb may help us to enter into the wonder that Jesus is risen, glorified and ever present.

Secondly, in my opinion, a miraculous explanation of the empty tomb and some other miracles cannot be entirely ruled out by scientific laws of nature. These are not, if I understand them correctly, unchangeable regulations of a closed system of nature. They are really just shorthand summaries of thousands of experiments and observations. So if you ask a scientist, 'Could this miracle happen?', he can only reply, if he confines himself to his own particular field of study, 'That is a question which as a scientist I am not competent to answer; the most I can say is that we have no such event in our scientific records.'

It would seem to me, as a Christian, that what we popularly call scientific laws are the normal sequences, as far as we can observe them, of God's way of working in nature. It is good perhaps that there are not too many miracles and that God's way is normally predictable. For if, for example, the law of gravity sometimes operated and sometimes did not, we should have some very curious games of football! But as God is God of all, there seems no reason to me, scientific or otherwise, why he should not depart from his normal sequences if some special reason required it. The resurrection of Jesus would seem to me such an exceptional, indeed a unique, occasion.

This leads me to my third preliminary matter. Science, in my view, does not rule out the possibility of Jesus' resurrection, but it does require us to weigh up the evidence carefully and to see to what explanation the evidence most likely points. In particular we have to investigate how wide a gap there is between the original happening and the evidence now available; clearly, as I said earlier, the narrower the gap, the more reliable is the evidence likely to be. Mark, the earliest gospel, was probably written some thirty years after the resurrection, though we must notice that the last eleven verses are not really part of this gospel at all, but are a postscript summary added much later on. The other three gospels were very probably written between 60 and 100 AD. Our earliest evidence, with a list of people the Risen Jesus appeared to, is in the fifteenth chapter of Paul's first letter to the Corinthians, written about fifteen years after the resurrection. Embedded in this chapter is a short, very significant passage:

For I delivered to you first of all that which I also received,

how that Christ died for our sins according to the Scriptures,

and that he was buried,

and that he was raised on the third day according to the Scriptures.

The first two verbs are almost technical terms for the handing down of a solemn formula. (In fact Paul uses this same pair of verbs when he hands on to them also the solemn account of Jesus at the last supper.) Then the next three phrases of our passage have the ring of a primitive formula or creed. The second and third of these phrases, 'and he was buried' and 'that he was raised on the third day', imply, I think, that the tomb was empty, even if it does not state it explicitly. It looks as if this three-phrased formula may well have been the Christian tradition handed down to Paul immediately after his conversion. If so, we have probably evidence for the empty tomb within a decade of Jesus' actual resurrection.

This evidence that the tomb was empty seems reliable enough for me. Next we must ask: '*How* was it that the tomb was empty on Easter morning?' My own considered opinion is that it was empty because Jesus' body had been raised, transformed and glorified. How else could the tomb be empty? Other suggested explanations are, I find, far less likely. I cannot think, as has been suggested, that a wild beast broke into the tomb and dragged the body away; or that the women and the apostles went to a wrong and unused tomb by mistake. Nor can I believe that some Jews stole the body, so as subsequently to mutilate it, for then they would never have let the apostles get away with their glad news that Jesus had risen from the tomb. Even more unlikely do I think the suggestion that the disciples removed the body and then exclaimed, 'Look, the tomb is empty; he must have risen.' Would they have suffered repeatedly and gladly for this claim, if they knew all the time that it was a deception? That would have been, I think, psychologically impossible.

The third pointer is the number of people who claimed that Jesus met them after the resurrection. It seems that the empty tomb by itself did not normally convince people that Jesus was alive again—it only left Mary Magdalene crying in despair; it was his coming to her and calling her by name that convinced her. We are told that Jesus met not Pilate nor the high priests nor any of the Pharisees, but only believers. Then is it possible that these so-called appearances were hallucinations, a kind of wishful thinking? I myself cannot believe so, for two reasons.

First, those who saw him were not expecting to see him. On the contrary, his coming was a surprise. Mary Magdalene at first thought he was a gardener. The disciples were not expecting him when he came to them inside the locked doors of their room. Thomas said he would never believe unless he could feel the scars of the wounds in the body of his Risen Master. When some of the disciples returned to their fishing on the lake of Galilee, they did not expect to see him nor indeed did they at first recognise him as he stood on the shore.

The second reason why I cannot believe that these appearances were hallucinations is that Paul, our earliest witness, says that Jesus appeared to over five hundred believers at once. It seems impossible to me that these five hundred should all suffer simultaneously from an hallucination. Paul adds that most of these five hundred are still alive. So it would be possible to cross-examine them. And we can see from the New Testament, especially from Paul's letters to the Corinthians, that the early Christians did not accept everything blindly, they were quite ready to cross-examine others in their search for the truth. Those who saw the Risen Jesus were not credulous enthusiasts.

For me and for many others these three pointers are enough to make us ready to go further and investigate what really happened at Easter. This investigation is not a kind of detective-story about what happened to the body. We are concerned with something much deeper. Paul affirmed that it was through God's mighty action in raising Jesus from the dead that God himself declared Jesus to be Son of God (Rom. 1.4). I might go a little further and say: 'It is as if all the Lord's teaching—for example his claim to have an unparalleled closeness to God and also to be our liberator—was written on a great parchment. Then when God raised Jesus from the dead, God set, as it were, his great red seal to this parchment and said, "All that is true. I give you my solemn word".' It is because God raised Jesus from the dead that we can be confident that Jesus is divine, that he can liberate us, and that he is our ever-present friend with us and within us by his Spirit.

No declaration could be more vital to us all. And our acceptance of Jesus Risen, like our grasp of the reality of God, begins, as Professor John Hick says, as 'an inferred entity' that gradually builds up into 'an experienced, personal presence'. We will now go on to see how this can really happen.

THE RISEN JESUS IN OUR LIVES TODAY

God has in Jesus and in his cross done all that is necessary to set in motion the liberating power of his love. But that liberation, as we saw in the previous chapter, only becomes effective in us when we respond personally to God in a love which expresses itself in confidence and *metanoia*, repentance. Similarly God has done all that is necessary to enable us to live day by day 'in the power of Jesus' resurrection'. But this power only goes into action in us, when we say 'Yes' by responding to him in love and by inviting him into our ordinary lives, with all their ups and downs.

This 'Yes', this personal decision, is vital and indispensable to becoming real Christians and our true selves. I know some people used not to see its necessity. They used to think that if you belonged to a predominantly Christian nation or lived in a Christian environment or a Christian congregation, you became more or less automatically a Christian. 'After all,' they would say, 'we're not Mohammedans or Hindus; still less are we atheists or agnostics, so presumably we must be Christians.' Or if boys and girls were sent to a good Christian school they would be expected to catch 'being a Christian' like measles. Or if you were well brought up in a good Christian family, then you supposed that somehow you were a Christian by descent. Yet it has been truly said, 'God has sons and daughters—but no grandsons and granddaughters.'

In New Testament times clearly people became followers of Jesus by deliberate choice. They had to decide to say 'Yes' to him. The first disciples gave up their fishing, they said 'Yes' to Jesus and followed him. Those three thousand men and women, Jews from many nations, who became Christians when they had heard Peter speak on the feast of Pentecost, had then to say, 'Yes, we believe that in Jesus our true Messiah has come, he has died for us and he has been raised from the dead; yes, we want him now to come into our lives.' When the pagans at Corinth and elsewhere became Christians, they said, 'Now in Jesus we see God as he really is, we believe Jesus died to set us free, and that God raised him from the dead; yes, we want him now to live in our lives.' Of course it is an advantage to live in a Christian country, in a Christian school and especially in a real Christian family, but we become the true disciples God means us to become—not by upbringing, but by our own choice, by saying 'Yes' to Jesus, and then going on meaning it.

A passage of the New Testament which once focussed this question for me personally and has done so for many of my friends, is a letter written by John, the author of the last book of the Bible, to the rather half-committed Christians at Laodicea in Asia Minor (Rev. 3.14-22). He sent it to them as a message he had received for them from the Risen Jesus:

Behold, I stand at the door and knock;
if any one hears my voice and opens the door,
I will come in to him and feast with him and he with
me.

These words were turned by Holman Hunt into his picture, 'The Light of the World'. I have often looked and pondered on the original in Keble College chapel, Oxford. There is, as you may know, a replica of it in St Paul's Cathedral, London and there are many reproductions of it. This pre-Raphaelite style of painting may not be in much favour now, but the symbolism of the picture still speaks to thousands. It is the Risen Jesus but he still has the scars of the wounds he bore for us, making clear his continuing love for us. He only knocks, he does not try to force himself in upon us. There is no latch or handle on the outside of the door. You and I are the person inside. He waits until we love enough to open the door. He knocks at all sorts of times, when we are at worship or in our personal prayers, often through the sight of human need or when we are meditating on the scriptures, or when we are out walking or reading a book—and sometimes quite unexpectedly.

Perhaps you may not have thought of being a Christian quite in these terms or of these words of Jesus as spoken personally to you. But as you read these pages slowly you might reflect on what this could mean to you—and through you to others whom you love or for whom you have some responsibility. It strikes me that the Lord does not ask us primarily to work hard or to speak well for him, but to love him. Service can be and sometimes is the expression of our love. But when in the gospels certain people said they had spoken on his behalf and had done wonderful things in his power, Jesus' reply was, 'I never knew you.' (Matt. 7.21-23). They had never opened their hearts to him and invited him to share their lives.

Then his invitation is a definite and individual one. Jesus is real, he is risen, he is ever present, actually with you. His words are not to a group of people—'if any *one* hears my voice...'—but just to you. I can remember a particular hour when he spoke these words to me.

I for one hesitated to say 'Yes', and I can well understand others who do so because they cannot see where it eventually will lead. But it is not a knock to be afraid of; it is not the knock of secret police in the middle of the night. It is a friend who stands outside and waits, One who loves us more than we can ever understand and whose purpose for us is the wisest and best. Even if asking him in involves future hardships, we know that God works all things for good to those who love him (Rom. 8.28); and that what he invites us to is primarily joy—'he will feast with me, and I with him.'

We needn't delay to say 'Yes' until a 'high moment' comes; it may be high or low key, perhaps not emotional at all. There's no pressure. It is simple action: at one moment the door was shut, the next it is open. Once the immediate issue is clear, it isn't rash to take the action—and I shouldn't like you to act rashly; but holding back may be cowardly. And further questions that arise can be solved as we go along, like the proverb some of us had to learn at school—*solvitur ambulando*. And if the hinges of this door are stiff and rusty, Jesus the Risen Lord is with you already to help you with his courage and power.

Perhaps you think that you have said your 'Yes' already. If you aren't sure, however, I'd recommend you to say a definite 'Yes' now. It will be like inking in your signature where you have first signed it in pencil. Perhaps you said a 'Yes' a long time ago, and your signature is rather faded; it would be worth while to go over it again with fresh ink. Or perhaps you may remember very clearly when and where you first said 'Yes' and you are still standing by it—and now are wondering what significance these pages may have for you.

Paul himself tells us to see in marriage an analogy for our relationship of love with God. Though some never marry and others have unhappy marriages, in important respects I find it a helpful comparison as long as we don't over-press it. We can follow it in our own way. There are of course other God-given close relationships. In these as well, there are both particularly decisive moments and also a gradual step-by-step deepening of mutual love. Neither a good marriage nor a deep friendship comes suddenly out of the blue. All sorts of questions need first to be honestly discussed, and so we gradually come to know one another more and more deeply.

Then for the married couple there is at last the great mutual 'Yes'. The bridegroom says in effect, 'Yes, I want to belong to you, and I ask you right into my heart and life'; and the bride says, 'Yes, I too desire to belong to you, and to welcome you right into my heart and life.' Then afterwards in their life together, many other issues will have to be worked out; deeper and deeper levels of themselves will be revealed to one another. Those who are happily married soon realise that the great 'Yes' has to be followed by a series of other 'yeses'. It is in this way that love grows stronger. Some of these 'yeses' may be hard, and they cannot be forced; there may be set-backs—but the 'yeses' need to go on. These will, I believe, always go on, for this life will not be long enough to discover together the full wonder of mutual love; for its plenitude eternity will be needed.

So it is, I am becoming increasingly convinced, between ourselves and God who comes to us in the Risen Jesus. I am always glad when I see my own friends and others saying 'Yes' to Jesus, sometimes in a very decisive way. But I know for myself and for them we shall need to go on re-affirming, extending and renewing our 'Yes'. Otherwise we shall just settle down into a kind of *arrested* relationship with the Lord. I must sadly admit that there have been such 'blockages', but by his mercy not too prolonged, in my own journey of life. For all of us there is this danger of love growing cold, of growing away from him. With every day that dawns I find I need to say at least a small 'Yes' to him. What is it that keeps many marriages warm, alive and growing? Isn't it those mutual *daily* words of gratitude, appreciation and understanding—those daily 'yeses'?

And we see this in the lives and personal writings of the great Christians, the real men and women of prayer. Few people could have more decisively and deeply said 'Yes' to the Risen Jesus than did Paul at that first meeting with him on the Damascus road. But years after he told his friends at Philippi that even now he had not yet 'arrived'. His 'yeses' were by no means completed.

It is not to be thought that I have already achieved all this. I have not reached perfection, but I press on, hoping to take hold of that for which Christ once took hold of me. My friends, I do not reckon myself to have got hold of it yet. All I can say is this: forgetting what is behind me, and reaching out for that which lies ahead, *I press on* towards the goal to win the prize which is God's call to the life above, in Christ Jesus (Phil. 3.12-14).

Lord, I wish to live on the right side of Easter.
I would like to know in myself the power of your resurrection.

I want to live in your own love and joy,
    not just for my own sake,
    but for the sake of others.
So help me, Lord, to open my life to you,
    and to go on keeping it open.

7 THE SPIRIT AND TRANSFORMATION

My last few years' reflecting and praying have led me to look over my life-journey. How many people, young and old, of various nations and races have helped and encouraged me. Some of them have never known how much they have meant to me. With Tennyson's Ulysses I could say: 'I am a part of all that I have met'. Looking back, I am now so grateful to them all.

One of them was a priest who was my 'guide, philosopher and friend' in the couple of years between the end of my university studies and my ordination. He was a man of exceptional human sensitivity, which grew out of his being a man of deep and disciplined prayer. He also had the knack of making straight, somewhat disconcerting remarks with such a twinkle in his eye that you couldn't take them wrong. In conversation one day I said something rather banal about the Holy Spirit; he looked straight at me and said: 'If anyone asks for the Holy Spirit, he is asking for trouble.'

The Spirit is the spirit of growth, the spirit of transformation. Growing in body, in spirit, in living together is, you will agree, indispensable, sometimes disturbing, sometimes exhilarating.

THE RISEN JESUS AND THE SPIRIT

When Jesus, God's self-disclosure, becomes the centre of our thinking and living, then so does the Holy Spirit. There is a close relationship in the New Testament between the Risen Jesus and the Spirit. Paul writes of God's sending the Spirit of Jesus his Son into our hearts. The Book of Acts says it was by the Spirit of Jesus that Paul was led in his missionary journeys (Acts 16.7). Yet the Risen Lord and the Spirit are not identified with one another. Jesus himself will send the Spirit: 'For if I do not go away, the Comforter will not come to you, but if I go, I will send him to you' (John 16.7). The first letter of John says that we can be sure that Jesus abides within us and adds: 'We know it from the Spirit he has given us' (1 John 3.24).

Some sixty years ago the well-known spiritual guide, Abbot Colomba Marmion, wrote: 'How many Christians of today know only the name of the Spirit and have experienced nothing of his power in their hearts.'

This is no longer so, thanks largely to the charismatic movement. I have met it in Australasia, Singapore, South Africa, in South and North America. I can see why people react strongly for it and against it. The charismatic Christians themselves know how much they need the Spirit's gift of discernment. I am a friend, if not a member, of the movement. I do not think I need write extensively about it here. Perhaps we could consider instead the even wider and more fundamental question, how the Spirit himself helps us to discover and grow into our true selves.

BECOMING OUR TRUE SELVES

I would like to gather together the hints I have already given about becoming our true selves and to see how they are linked to the Holy Spirit of growth and transformation. This for me is exploring new ground.

Becoming our true selves means letting ourselves be transformed through the Holy Spirit, in his light and by his power. This is not self-culture. It is not modelling ourselves on anyone else. That would be artificial. Even Jesus came not to be our model, but our lover and liberator. The Spirit will help us to discover and to become who God intends *us* to be.

Within his great human family God in his love means us to be different from one another. That wise guide, Friedrich von Hügel, wrote to his niece, 'Souls are never dittos.' Good parents try to love their children—difficult as it sometimes is—equally *but* differently, so that they

79

can grow to be their true and different selves. As we saw, it is difficult for us to realise that the infinite God could love us all in this personal, individual way. Without Jesus we probably couldn't believe it. But we are seeing all through this book that God's way of loving now is Jesus' way of loving in the gospels, a loving that adjusts itself to each individual's *real* needs. And also because true love never stands still, God's purpose for each of us is an ever-unfolding purpose.

This transformation is not a solo thing. Even the Holy Spirit can transform only within the setting of God's great family. The Spirit does this normally through our warm, caring relationships, rooted and grounded in a living trustful relation with God.

This transformation is usually a quiet growth, though there are certainly breakthroughs. In a late cold English spring the tender green leaves open on the various trees at different paces and slowly; but with a few sunny days there is a marvellous efflorescence. So it is with us. And our growth through the Spirit is growth from within, like the leaves, blossom and fruit. We don't tie apples on to trees; they grow. Love, joy and peace, Paul tells us, are the *fruit* of the Spirit. He produces the fruit. But the tree has to be pruned.

HOW HAVE THINGS GONE WRONG?

I often ask myself—and perhaps you do too—'Why aren't things better than they are?' They could be—in spite of the fallenness of our human nature and the cosmic powers of evil.

For we are all born with the beginnings of these three marvellous gifts—the gift of responding to God's love, the gift of being able to love one another and the gift of a proper appreciation and love of ourselves. We see these gifts in Jesus, in his own personality and in his teaching. They could be so good for us, for our neighbours and for human society. Why aren't they developed and put into action? For two reasons; we don't talk about them, and we don't live them.

First, many men and women of today don't recognise these capacities in themselves or in others, partly because we ourselves don't talk about these gifts. I don't mean that we should do 'religious propaganda'. But ought we not to talk more often than we do about people and these gifts of theirs—not in a wooden way, but imaginatively? Anyway I intend now to devote my ministry to this line, and that is why I am writing this book. Ought not this approach to colour the way we discuss the news and current affairs? The future of our society is, I think, now in the balance.

But—and it is a big 'but'—there is all the difference between people's accepting intellectually that we possess this triple gift of love, and feeling it 'click' into our lives. We may accept all this language about really knowing and loving God, our neighbours and ourselves, but it cannot grip us and work within us, unless we have ourselves experienced friendship and love. 'Anyone who doesn't love can't know God', says the first letter of John. To know God's love only theoretically is like our going to Paris with a knowledge of French grammar, a vocabulary of fifty words and no idea of French pronunciation; we should not 'relate' well.

Secondly, we can't talk about it, because we don't live it. To live it means to go out, as Jesus did, with love to make contact with all sorts of people. Often we want to, but can't. We hide behind what we call our shyness. I know what it is like. But we can't care without involvement. Hand must go with heart. 'None of that cold, distant charity', Charles de Foucauld used to say. Sometimes we are afraid of human warmth and of the human body, its joy and tears. 'He lived at a certain distance from his body', James Joyce said of one of his characters. It was not so with Jesus. He held the children in his arms. He cried so much at Lazarus' death that people said, 'See how he loved him.'

The causes of our being ill-at-ease with some people, which we vaguely call shyness, are complex. We are all different. We each have our personal life-story. But among other reasons for this shyness there are often a rather 'cool' upbringing, an over-intellectualised and competitive education and the long-term influence of others' attitudes and words—sometimes chance words.

Then let us begin by looking back at our earliest years. I have been one of the lucky ones, but I feel deeply for those who have been less fortunate. Clearly God means us to be born into and welcomed into an atmosphere of love. Tiny children are susceptible to atmosphere long before they can say a word. I have known a small baby react to tension in the home by going off his food and being restless. We need not only to be loved, but to feel loved unconditionally. This and the right interplay of family affections are the foundation for those deep trusting relationships we shall need to make and maintain during the rest of our lives. One of the most damaging things I ever heard a young mother say to her child— though she was greatly provoked—was: 'If you do that again, Mummy won't love you.' Such early threats of rejection, withdrawal of love, for whatever reason, can undermine our feelings of security, blunt our capacity for going out in love to others, and distort our ideas of God.

How many religious people have come through such experiences into the gloom of scrupulosity and self-belittlement. They regard God as a harsh maker of rules whose favour has to be earned by keeping them strictly. How different from Jesus' parable of the prodigal father, prodigal in his love. Before his son could reach the house or make a full apology, the father ran down the road, embraced him and kissed him. He didn't say, 'Show me you have turned over a new leaf, settle down and work and then I will reinstate you.' On the contrary, he said, 'We'll have the best party we can put on, and we'll have it at once.' Many practising Christians may, to be honest, feel this welcome was either imprudent or too good to be true; but that is to have no heart-knowledge of the parable; and maybe they have not experienced this kind of love. Don't get me wrong. I do not mean God is indifferent about whether we are growing into our true selves or not; but he wants our effort to spring not from anxious fear, but from gratitude and love: 'Father, thank you more than I can say, and now I want to grow into what you wish me to be, and may your Holy Spirit work within me.'

God's love, like all good love, is not soft or indulgent, but constant and predictable. We all need to know where we stand. That is why mutual commitment is looked for in all deep human relationships. 'Is it for always?', we ask; and we need to hear the word 'Yes'.

Next, let us consider our education. On reflection I find traditional English education, good and thorough as it has been in many ways, has had the effect on some of us of deflecting, repressing or delaying our attempts to discover our true selves. First, great pressure has been put on us to 'conform' to the ideas of the teaching authorities or of our peer group. Secondly, in the competitiveness of the system we often put personal ambition first—I know I did—and become insensitive to the needs of those around us. I am still committed to high academic standards, but not at the cost of our humanness. Yet we must not be severe on our parents and teachers; they were often devoted to their tasks, but almost inevitably men and women of their age. Any resentment we may feel will do no good.

Then also there are other long-term influences which may have mis-shaped our personalities. Up to a point these have been our fault. We have sometimes put our own enjoyment first or have just followed some craze or cliché of the day. Other people's asides, *obiter dicta*, can also easily distort our lives for a time. I remember a games master whom I rather admired as boys do. He liked to turn out a neat phrase. One of his oversimplifications I took too seriously: 'Men are concerned with things, women with people; men with achievements, women with feelings.' The result was that art, music, poetry and real personal relationships were something of a closed book to me for years. I said I hadn't time for them; and certainly I was absorbed in my scientific studies. My ambition and heart were there.

But *love* is what we are all created for; this is what real life is about. Paul writes in chapter thirteen of his first letter to the Corinthians almost a poem on what real love is; and then he goes on to say, 'Put love first' (1 Cor. 14.1).

As we look around us, we see how many men and women, old and young, lack confidence, have become mis-shapen, been damaged by sarcasm and harshness, hurt—wounded is perhaps not too strong a word—by hardness in their lives. Some of these wounds are deep and go back a long way—though now often hidden behind an apparently assured character. What can be done about all this? Not very much by ourselves and our will-power. Healing only comes through love, real love.

THE HEALING POWER OF LOVE

Real love, both human and divine,—so Dr Jack Dominian, a Roman Catholic psychiatrist, says—gives us first inner assurance, next sustains us, then heals us and also enables us to grow into our true selves.

Perhaps many of us can see this more clearly at first with human affection. I speak of real friendships. These often take years to make. They require generosity in giving and gladness in receiving on both sides. But when a friend really comes to love us, we feel we can 'be' ourselves in his company, we begin to be distinct, to value ourselves. We find we can do this just because a close friend cares for us ourselves, not for anything that can be got out of us, not for any particular gifts we may have or for any gaps there are in our makeup. 'I love you, not for your gifts, nor for your needs, but just for yourself.' This is how we learn to appreciate and not to undervalue ourselves any more. That is often an important first step.

Yet even after this step we often find it hard not to slip back into discouragement, or not to be afraid of future possible difficulties. But a true friend sustains us, keeps us going on. Then with time this new affection begins to heal those old hurts and wounds inflicted by lack of love. This healing may not be easy. We may need medical and other counselling as well. But genuine love heals. As we are healed, we grow. We become our true selves, as God intended. This takes a lifetime—and more.

But if we expect our friends to give us all the love and support we need in these ways, we may be asking them to do more than they can manage; and perhaps this is one reason why some marriages and friendships break down. We are so made that we normally need both divine and human resources of love.

Yet there is no real separation between the divine and human love. Jesus himself clearly loved with human affection. We remember his tears at Lazarus' grave. His human affection, as we saw, became the channel of God's love; and so can ours.

For the divine love helps us in the same way as human love. Let us again watch and meditate on God's love in Jesus doing those same four things.

First, Jesus by his love gives people inner self-assurance. You may remember the man blind from birth. No one bothers about him, even his parents repudiate him. He can do nothing but beg, for he has lost all self-esteem. Jesus in his love gives him not only sight but also self-assurance. The healed man then stands up to the fierce cross-examination by the Pharisees and their excommunication of him. This is what divine love begins to do for him. It not only enables him to see, but—quite as important—it gives him courage to stand on his own feet (John 9).

Then Jesus' love not only gives hope to the hopeless, he also sustains them in confidence. Jairus comes to Jesus in his moment of need. His twelve-year-old daughter is dying. Jesus says, 'I'll come at once.' But then he is delayed, for a woman suffering from haemorrhage demands his time. Jesus understands and knows how desperate Jairus is now feeling. He turns to him and sustains his confidence. 'Don't be afraid; only have faith'. And soon Jairus' daughter was restored to him.

Next, Jesus' love heals—inwardly and outwardly. To the paralysed man, brought on a stretcher, Jesus says, 'Your sins are forgiven', as well as 'Pick up your stretcher and walk.' Then after healing Jesus' love brings us to maturity as our true selves. He healed Mary Magdalene of some deep infirmity—'seven devils came out of her', the gospel says. Then he let her and others journey with him. Her response of love grew. Then on Good Friday, when nearly all his followers had fled for their lives, she stood by him at his cross in mature love.

It is *through the Holy Spirit* that this strengthening, sustaining, healing, maturing love of God, which we see in Jesus, comes to penetrate our personalities. 'God's love has been poured into our hearts through the Holy Spirit who has been given to us' (Rom. 5.5). Then, says Paul, 'Walk *in* the Spirit' (Gal. 5.16).

The Spirit comes to us like the wind. 'The wind blows where it wills'. So the Spirit can take us by surprise and lead us in unexpected ways. Sometimes he gives us a quiet impulse, like a gentle breeze, 'a still small voice', or as it is literally in the Hebrew, 'a sound of gentle stillness' (1 Kings 19.12). But sometimes he comes to us like a boisterous gale, as he came to the apostles on the feast of Pentecost. Right across the Christian centuries, and now in the charismatic movement, he comes with a joyful turbulence. All of us are agreed, because so much is at stake, that we need to be able to discern what is genuinely the Spirit's own influence.

THE HOLY SPIRIT AND THE SCRIPTURES

The Holy Spirit is today re-awakening in us a new *love* of the scriptures. This is happening partly through the charismatic movement, and also through the liturgical movement, which in nearly all the Churches is deepening the spirit and wonder of our worship and prayer.

At first sight the Bible may look remote to men and women of today. But when we see that the heart of the Bible is the coming of God's love for us in Jesus, it begins to make sense. And it becomes even more interesting when the Bible itself makes clear that this coming of God in Jesus is not only the centre of its span of history, but is also the key to our own personal maturity; for, as St Bernard said: '*In giving himself to me, God has made me myself.*'

The high point of the Bible is obviously the gospels, and these show us Jesus, as his first followers saw him and responded to him; the rest of the New Testament spells out his cosmic significance; the Old Testament gives us his cultural and religious background. Yet the Bible isn't a book at all. As we open it, we walk into a vast library. The actual writing of its books spanned at least a thousand years; selecting this collection was a complex, long-drawn-out process; and to find our way about this library we need advice and a guide. For there is in it a baffling variety, from the cynical Ecclesiastes, through the love-poetry of the Song of Songs to the bizarre imagery in the Book of Revelation. It reminds me of how baffling—and disturbing—I have at times found the experience of God's love.

Some of the books explicitly claim that they, or sayings incorporated in them, were inspired by God. The second letter to Timothy says: 'All scripture is inspired by God and profitable for teaching' (2 Tim. 3.16); but this cannot mean that the genealogical tables of the Old Testament, to take an extreme example, are inspired just in the same way as the letters of John or Paul. There are also of course other inspired writings, like *The Imitation of Christ* or *Pilgrim's Progress*; and these too we can use for prayerful reading or sometimes in our worship together. But the biblical writings are the inspired foundation-documents both for our believing and our praying, because of their close relation to God's coming to us in Jesus.

It is because of this special relationship and inspiration that I have come to see these books very much as I see Jesus himself. He is genuinely human and yet through his humanity shines the divine light and love. So it is, I think, with the scriptures. That is why we should, I suggest, use them in two ways, though I would not like to draw a sharp line between them; I'll call these ways bible-reading and bible-praying respectively. Let me try to explain. If you receive a letter from a close friend, it does two things for you, not one. It first gives you the news of what your friend has been doing, and that of course interests you. But that is only half the purpose of the letter; it also brings your friend and his affection right to you. A letter of this kind is a 'written meeting'; and so we keep these letters and read them over again—as we do the gospels.

We can never understand scripture without systematic *bible-reading*. What was the human setting of these books? These words did not fall from heaven; one book, for example, came very much through the mind and heart of Paul, a rather volatile man, to a group of Christians, his warm friends at Philippi, with their particular problems. I'd like to suggest two background books, Bernard Anderson's clear, well-illustrated *Living World of the Old Testament* (Longmans) and W. D. Davies' *Invitation to the New Testament* (SPCK), written for Rachel, his teenage daughter. Then perhaps you could, alone or with others, read a book of the Bible with a short recommended commentary for an hour once a week. There are also daily bible-notes from the Bible Reading Fellowship or from the more conservative Scripture Union. These notes are a kind of halfway-house between bible-reading and bible-praying.

In *bible-praying*, on the other hand, we do not set out to learn anything new. We wish not to learn but to meet. This is why for bible-praying, as distinct from bible-reading, I usually go through the gospels again and again, just a few verses a day. I don't get tired of them just as I never get tired of my friends' letters. Occasionally I use other parts of the scriptures in the same way, like Psalm 23 or some verses from the epistles about Jesus. I try to do this early in the morning. As Dietrich Bonhoeffer used to say: 'Talk to Jesus first before you talk to other people.' These few minutes are often not particularly emotional. But if I miss them, it is for me like missing the visit of a friend. And if I leave them out for a few days, I begin to lose my sensitivity to Jesus and also to my neighbours. This, of course, is rather serious. Perhaps you would like to arrange a few

minutes' quiet meeting like this either early in the morning or at some other time in the day when you are fairly
sure of not being interrupted. I will expand later on what
I have sketched here.

PONDERING AND PRAISING

After bible-reading or bible-praying we may feel drawn
by the Spirit to pondering or to praising. This pondering
on the implications of the passage may be quite important; and in the gospels we read of Mary pondering
Jesus' words in her heart. We must not think that we are
wasting our time in prayer if we are not definitely thinking things out and putting our reflections into words.
Prayer is not being busy. It is more like to two close
friends being glad to be with one another; they just don't
look at the clock. Certainly the heart of our bible-
praying is simply being *with* the Lord, deeply aware of
his presence and receptive to his love. This is of course
not at all to say that this quiet prayer will not have clear
and definite results in our everyday lives.

   At other times we shall be led by the Spirit into thanking and praising God. This is primarily expressing our
love for God, rather as we express our love to those who
are dearest to us. Our minds and hearts are centred on
God. We are responding with our love to his infinite
love. The scriptures, especially some of the psalms, call
us to praise God. This praising God is meaning more and
more to me. One day I must try to write more about it.

   We praise God just because we love him. But we discover that this praising God has often a wonderful—
though quite incidental—effect on ourselves; it is, if I
may say so, quietly joyful and therapeutic, so good for
us. C. S. Lewis used to say, 'Praise is an audible sign of
health'; and he added, 'The most balanced and capa-
cious minds praise most, while cranks, misfits and mal-
contents praise least.' When I praise God, I often do so
in unpremeditated words of my own. Sometimes words
of the liturgy or of the psalms come spontaneously to my
lips.

My heart danceth for joy,
And in my song will I praise him.
And at times as my praising grows deeper, it becomes quite wordless; and I am happy that it should be so.

Some friends of mine in the charismatic movement tell me that when in praising God they—as they put it—'run out of words', they find themselves praising God inarticulately 'in tongues'. They tell me also that 'praying in tongues' has a way of deepening their love and understanding of others.

I remember a friend of mine, a priest, not at that time a member of the charismatic movement, telling me an experience of his. He had been to a difficult meeting one morning. There had been hard words and frayed nerves. He returned to his house discouraged and went into his study to pray. As he prayed quietly and trustfully, 'Abba, Father, Abba, Father', he lost all sense of time— indeed later his wife asked him what he had been doing and why he had been so long—and found himself praying *sotto voce* 'in tongues'. Not only did this remove his tension, but—as other people remarked—it wonderfully deepened his sensitivity and his ability 'to get alongside others'.

Clearly some Christians in New Testament times spoke 'in tongues'. Paul did himself; and he also said that it is a gift which the Spirit gives to some, but not to all. And down the centuries many men and women of prayer have not received this gift. Certainly we all should try to hold ourselves open to receive whatever gifts the Spirit may wish to give us. But we desire the Giver more than any of his gifts, and the Giver himself is Love.

BODY AND SPIRIT

'God forbid that I should separate', says that short classic of quiet and contemplative prayer, *The Cloud of Unknowing*, 'what God has joined together—the body and the spirit.' We are now recovering our sense of wonder that God has so marvellously made and linked together our bodies and our spirits, and that he created us with such potentialities for friendship and love, human and divine. He has given us all these gifts, so that we can help one another to discover and become our true selves—and so best care for our neighbours in the world. Even the best of gifts can of course be misused. But we see Jesus using them all so constructively.

Yet even in New Testament times there had begun to creep into the Church an oriental dualism. It implied that the spirit alone was good and really mattered. It treated the human body and its feelings as second rate and not far short of evil. Until about a generation ago this erroneous outlook was widespread in the Church and in much of western society. Some of its unfortunate consequences are still with us. But it is repudiated by modern Christian movements like the charismatic and liturgical renewals. The new wedding liturgy in the Church of England is an example; it speaks of marriage as a gift from God to the husband and wife so that 'with delight and tenderness they may know each other in love, and, through the joy of their bodily union, may strengthen the union of their hearts and lives.' I must leave you to think out all the implications of this renewed positive appreciation of our bodies and spirits; and I will just mention two.

The first is that both our bodies as well as our spirits should be as much involved in prayer and worship as they are in friendship and love. A good posture of the body and slow deep breathing can make some of us more ready for personal prayer. Gestures of reverence can also deepen the inward spirit of prayer.

For corporate worship it is a help to have a clear, easily appreciated plan of the service to follow, but within this outline we need plenty of spontaneity and variety, of movement and joy. This was true of Hebrew worship.

Praise him with the timbrel and dances,
Praise him upon the strings and pipe.

This must have been part of the background of Jesus' own life of worship and prayer.

Our worship is not just individuals praying in one building. We are an orchestra of praise and love. To help us to realise this, some people are now glad to exchange with one another a sign of greeting and peace. Of course we must be sensitive to others' temperaments and backgrounds; and the latest fashions in worship are not always the best. But prayer and worship should help us gently to discover our true selves in body and feelings as well as in spirit. We remember again that Jesus did not suppress his joys or his tears.

The second implication of the new appreciation of our bodies is our renewed concern about healing in the life of love and of prayer. Jesus healed people's bodies by cures, not only their spirits by forgiveness. Healing has all through the centuries had its place in the life of the Church. I have laid hands on the sick throughout my own ministry, and often with wonderful blessings. Unfortunately this healing ministry has often been neglected. We are grateful that the charismatic movement is now helping to restore it to its full place in the Church. I myself welcome this very much. Wholeness of life is the hope we set before us as we mature to become our true selves.

As a consequence I recognise how important it is for me—and perhaps for you too—to keep, as Paul would say, 'in training' and alert in heart and mind. I see this as a vital element in my loving and helping those to whom God sends me. Perhaps even more I now regard it as a way of expressing my love for God and my deep gratitude to him for so wonderfully creating me in body, mind and spirit.

There are a few possible misunderstandings which we should avoid. First, some people, who have this interest in spiritual healing, seem to say to us that, if we had enough faith, we shouldn't have illnesses. So they may make us feel needlessly guilty; and I'm sorry about that. We should always, I grant, seek for spiritual healing; and we should—by quiet prayer and the help of the Spirit— be growing in trust in God. Our confidence, let us notice, is confidence not in techniques of prayer but in God himself, who comes to us in Jesus.

But accidents and epidemics, strain and violence are

part of our world. So pain and illness come to nearly all of us. We turn to God with trust and love. But usually our troubles are not taken away at once. We need to ask the Holy Spirit to help us, at least for a time, to live with them as patiently, as bravely, as joyfully as we can. I know from my own experience how difficult this can be.

We shall also, as the years pass, have to prepare and adjust ourselves to the inevitable wearing out of our minds and bodies; though we must try to preserve our youthfulness of spirit, as his abbot said of Thomas Merton, that lively-minded monk and spiritual guide, who died at fifty-three. 'Even if he had lived to be a hundred, he would have died a young man.'

So secondly, we should always keep ourselves open to spiritual healing, linked with the best medical care we can find. God uses both and they help one another. When spiritual help, for example, begins to remove negative emotions like fear and jealousy, it builds up our physical vitality. Our spirit and body are so closely intertwined. Our spirit does not just live in the body, like a driver seated in a car. We are spirit-and-body-in-one.

Thirdly, we may, as I have said, find in spite of all our persistent search for health and of our trustful praying that we cannot—at least at present—get rid of some physical or emotional or psychological weakness. What then? I well understand from experience how depressed and discouraged we may feel. But we need specially at these times to remember how close Jesus is to us. He understands and helps us, for he himself learned how to live through his sorrows and sufferings. Indeed the letter to the Hebrews says, 'Since he himself has passed through the test of suffering, he is able to help those who are meeting their test now' (Hebrews 2.18).

Paul too, we remember, found out how to live with his affliction; and he in time discovered that this actually helped him to grow spiritually, because it kept him aware of his hour-by-hour dependence on God's love, and so he could say, 'When I am weak, then I am strong' (2 Cor. 12.7-10). Eventually Paul realised how he could actually rejoice in his sufferings (Col. 1.24). To him they

93

were no longer a frustration, but rather a channel to bring God's love to others. For he could humbly and confidently offer up his sufferings along with his prayers to God in union with the perfect offering of Jesus' love, so as to bring blessings to his friends and others.

All the time we must try to be aware of the presence with us of Jesus the great strengthener and healer. Yet strangely how often Jesus told those whom he had healed not to speak about it. For he wished to be known not chiefly as the great healer—but as the great lover.

THE HOLY SPIRIT AND DISCERNMENT

In all these matters how much, as our friends in the char-ismatic renewal remind us, we need the Holy Spirit as the Spirit, not only of growth and transformation, but also of wisdom and discernment. We can be sure that he will progressively guide us, if we remain open to him.

First he leads us to think out our own decisions. As he helps us to mature into our true selves, so we become more sensitive to others and also more objective. So Paul, as he writes about our life in the Spirit, can say to us: 'Be grown-up in your thinking' (1 Cor. 14.20).

Next, the Holy Spirit does not mean us to be solitary, lonely pilgrims. He gives us experienced guides so that we can learn from those who have gone before us. Later on, as we ourselves travel further, he may entrust to us the responsibility of helping others. All guides need wide sympathies. One of the most discerning of them, Augustine Baker, gives us a necessary warning: 'A spiritual guide is not to teach his own way, but to help others to discover what is the best way for them.' So we should have a broad knowledge of these other ways. My short books, *Guides to Hidden Springs* and *Twentieth-Century Men of Prayer*, could introduce you to a wide variety of men and women who found very different ways through difficulties to real maturity of loving and praying. All these guides are intended to bring us to be led by the supreme guide and discerner of our hearts, the Holy Spirit himself.

Then, the Holy Spirit may help us to find a small group of friends with whom we can share humbly both our insights and disappointments. None of us by ourselves can grasp all the facets of the wonder of God's love for us. It is only in company with all God's people, the letter to the Ephesians tells us, that we shall grasp and know 'What is the breadth and length and height and depth of the love of Christ' (Eph. 3.18-19).

This is what the Church, the Christian community, should be doing for us. So we will turn to the Church, which can be to us such a disappointment or such an inspiration.

But now a moment of reflection on our theme as it has developed so far:

Help me, Lord, to build my life on sound foundations
   on your unalterable love for us in Jesus,
   on true humanness—of body as well as of spirit—
         which we see in Jesus,
   on the sureness of the liberating love which he
         brings to us,
   on the reality of the Holy Spirit in our hearts,
   the Spirit of growth and transformation.
Spirit of Jesus, show me how to go on from where I
         am now.

8   LIVING AND WORSHIPPING TOGETHER

'The Church we desire for ourselves and for everyone is', Cardinal Marty, a recent Archbishop of Paris, said, 'the embodiment of God's love for us.' As God's love disclosed in Jesus comes to mean more to us, so we should naturally turn with more expectancy to the Church of Jesus Christ, which the New Testament calls his bride. But many people in the west today are disappointed with the Church. It seems remote from real life. Its congregations are sometimes small and rather elderly, its worship dull and uninspiring. Overburdened with a top-heavy bureaucracy, it is often turned in on its own minor concerns. Yet to have a fair, balanced picture, we must remember the Church in other places is alive and growing fast, as I have seen myself in South America, in parts of the East like Indonesia, Singapore and Korea, and in Africa. For example, in the twenty years after 1952 the number of Roman Catholics in Africa increased from twelve and a half million to thirty-six million, and the number of African priests from fourteen hundred to four thousand two hundred. In the west too we see genuine signs of new life—the Focolari movement, Taizé the Little Brothers and Sisters of Jesus, dynamically fresh groups and communities.

> For while the tired waves, vainly breaking,
>   Seem here no painful inch to gain,
> Far back, through creeks and inlets making,
>   Comes silent, flooding in, the main.

If the Church near where we live seems a bit moribund, we shall not help it by standing on its fringe; and perhaps we should use a prayer, much loved in Africa: 'Lord, renew your Church—beginning with me.'

The Church is not an optional extra. We need it. We cannot mature into our true selves without fellowship both with God and also with one another—and that is what the Church is for. Paul explains in his letter to the Colossians that his life-work is to help men and women to become 'mature in Christ' (Col. 1.28 RSV); and he there shows that to become mature we need to marvel at the mystery of Jesus and to live in the fellowship of the Church of which Jesus is the head and the heart.

This is the message of the whole of the New Testament. When the first disciples left their fishing-boats and answered the call, 'Come, follow me'—rather like our 'Yes' to our Risen Lord—Jesus linked them at once not only with himself but with one another in the fellowship of the twelve. Later Jesus made them part of the wider fellowship of seventy, whom he sent out as the agents of his love; and also he brought Mary Magdalene and other women into the company of his followers. Christian maturity means our learning how to live with one another, as well as with the Lord. This fellowship continued to grow. Just before the feast of Pentecost the disciples were about a hundred and twenty; then on that day three thousand, as we have seen, were added to their number, and many of these had come to Jerusalem from around the Mediterranean world. As soon as God's love in Jesus becomes real to us, at once—although we may not realise it—we become members of a community that circles the globe.

We have to say 'Yes' to Jesus individually by ourselves. No one can do it for us. It may well be a very quiet experience, while we are in a retreat or while we are reading a book, It came to C. S. Lewis as he was by himself, riding on a bus. But quite soon we feel like telling some of our friends. It is like falling in love. We can't keep it to ourselves. We want to share our joy with others—with others who will understand. This is how small Christian groups form. And in them we may feel quite close to the first Christian community in the Acts of the Apostles, 'whose faith had drawn them together' and who 'shared their meals with unaffected joy' (Acts 2.44, 46). This is what God intends his Church to be.

But saying 'Yes' to Jesus brings us not only into a group of Christian friends. It links us to our local Church; if it is lively, it will help us; if not, it may need us. It makes us also members of a worldwide community. We need these wide horizons, if we are going to mature into our true selves. And if we are really drawn near to Christ, we are by that very fact linked across all frontiers to others who are close to him. As Paul says, 'There is no such thing as Jew and Greek, slave and freeman, male and female; for you are all *one person* in Christ Jesus' (Gal. 3.28). As we shall see in our next chapter, the Christian can never care only for his own small circle.

LOVING TOGETHER—THE BRIDE OF CHRIST

Paul calls this worldwide fellowship 'the Bride of Christ'. No phrase could better express our closeness to our Risen Jesus. In the New Testament it speaks primarily of the dependence of the whole Church on Christ and of its loyalty to him. But these magnificent words will have no substance, no reality, unless we have a kind of one-to-one bridal love and loyalty to our Lord. We wonder at his immense, unchangeable love for us; we want with the help of his Spirit always to respond to him, and we want our love to grow. Marriage isn't just living together; it is *growing* in love. So prayer is growing in love.

We long to grow, although we know it is not going to be always a gentle climb together. That is why in the Anglican wedding service husband and wife rejoice to take and hold one another in love 'for better, for worse, for richer, for poorer, in sickness and in health'. This is so in all deep, true relationships—and so in our love for God. The course of true love doesn't run smooth—and often in quite unanticipated ways. Yet love grows deeper, when those who love find out how to give needed support to one another. It was, as we have noticed, when Paul had to endure his 'thorn in the flesh' that he was most conscious of the love and power of God. Similarly in the first letter of Peter Christians were told to try to rejoice in their sufferings during the coming persecution, because in this way they would have the privilege of sharing in the work and sufferings of Christ, which bring God's liberating love to others. 'My dear friends, do not be bewildered by the fiery ordeal that is upon you, as though it were something extraordinary. It gives you a share in Christ's sufferings, and that is a cause of joy' (1 Pet. 4.12-13).

And today many Christians are suffering persecution with such steadfastness, courage and even joy. And, nearer home, how tough life can be I know from my own experience and from the much harder experience of some of my friends. And there can be no easy solutions—but we can rely on the companionship of Jesus. He understands our situation and he strengthens us by his Spirit. He himself went through with such love and courage his great sufferings to become our liberator.

He himself said to those of us who wish to be his friends and lovers, 'If anyone wants to come with me, he must *forget self*, take up his cross every day, and follow me' (Luke 9.23). This 'forgetting self' does not mean that we must belittle ourselves or pity ourselves; not at all, for we are men and women created 'in the image of God'. 'Forgetting ourselves' means that *metanoia*, that personal Copernican revolution, by which the centre of gravity of our lives is shifted to God and his glory from ourselves and our own convenience.

Jesus calls us to share his way of living, his way of carrying his cross in love; and he calls us to follow him, to be with him every day as his friends. Our sufferings may be physical or mental or it may be the relentless presure of our daily life as well. It was so for Paul: 'the responsibility that weighs on me every day, my anxious concern for all our congregations' (2 Cor. 11.28). Paul himself found that this was *the* way to love Jesus. He discovered that we experience the power and joy of Jesus' resurrection within us only in proportion as we share with him in his sufferings (Phil. 3.10). If every day is for us Good

Friday, then every day is Easter day. It is a sign that you love someone, when you are ready for love's sake to enter into their sufferings. This is the daily road for Jesus' friends and lovers; and it is our daily maturing into our true selves.

Because the Church is the Bride of Christ, it is also the Body of Christ. Bride and bridegroom belong in heart and in body to one another; and they rejoice in this kind of belonging more and more, as their loving grows. If the whole Church is Christ's Body, then each one of us is called to be a particular part of his body to carry his love and care to others. For, as Teresa of Avila, a realist and woman of prayer, put it:

> Christ has no body now on earth but yours, no hands but yours and no feet but yours.
> Yours are the eyes through which Christ looks out with compassion on the world.
> Yours are the feet with which he is to go about doing good.
> Yours are the hands with which he is to bless men now.

And what does our Risen Jesus wish to do through us? The first thing, the most obvious and most forgotten thing, is that he wishes to do *through* us what he has begun to do *in* us. He has, through bringing us the divine love, begun already to help us to mature into our true selves. Now he wishes us, by bringing to others his love, to help them to grow to their real maturity—though they may as yet be unaware of this their deepest need. And how shall we do this?

Again, I do not mean that we must always be talking about religion. We must first learn to look at everyone with the compassionate eyes of Christ. Then we should be training ourselves to explain to others how we now look at life: 'Be ready at all times to answer anyone who asks you to explain the hope you have in you, but do it with gentleness and respect' (1 Pet. 3.15-16). The kind of things we are considering in this book should, through reflection and meditation, become so much part of ourselves, that we can share them persuasively with others.

This is something which, I think, almost everyone can do. But in each small group or local church some may be particularly gifted. We must therefore each try to discover our real selves and our particular potentialities, and then develop them. We should never envy those who are more gifted that we are. For the influence of a Christian group is so much weakened when people sense within it jealousy and party-spirit. The New Testament and our own experience show how difficult it is for sincere people to get on with one another. For each one of us God has a special niche, calling and responsibility. How often we should remember this with gratitude in our daily prayers. I never cease to wonder and to thank God how—in spite of my missing many opportunities—he has led me step by step to my present responsibilities; and it is clearly much more his doing than mine. Perhaps you too would like to trace how he has also led you in spite of many things which seem inexplicable.

Then as we reflect on how the Lord wishes to use all of us as his body in our daily work and friendships, we must never think that we have 'arrived'. Our call from God has still to unfold into its deepest significance. It is true that God may have called us at special moments in the past, when we have said some great 'Yes' to him. But Paul speaks of God, not as one who has called us, but who calls us, and goes on calling us, closer to himself and nearer to others; and God is faithful and reliable, and he will give us the new love and strength we shall require. 'He who *calls* you will do it, because he is faithful' (1 Thess. 5.24). Often it is during worship that he calls us to his service and enables us to do it.

WORSHIPPING TOGETHER

Recently I was invited to one of our large, residential

public schools and I enjoyed sharing for a week the lives of the boys and girls at their meals, in their houses and classrooms and on their playing fields. I talked with them on the lines of this book, though naturally in a different key. For this theme meets a deep need, I am sure, at *every* stage of our lives if expressed in an appropriate way. We had plenty of discussions and also short—very short by adult standards—silent times for reflection or meditation.

On the last night a senior boy said to me: 'You made it all sound so real; but usually school chapel is such a bore.' I felt a bit flattered, but their chapel wasn't really all that boring. Yet there was something in what he said; and, frankly speaking, though I am a priest, I've sometimes found church worship rather dull—and haven't you? I can think of at least four reasons why.

First, we are expected to be there, but we aren't really in it. It is something which somebody else has 'put on'. As long as we feel this, it stunts our personal growth. Don't think I'm against regular, even frequent, worship. But we must first get our motivation right. I'll come back to that in a moment.

Secondly, we often use far too many words. A newcomer to worship said to me recently, 'You feed too many ideas into us. Before we've time to be quiet and absorb one thing, you're away on another.' If I were a parish-priest again, I would not impose my policy on others, but I'd discuss it and see what my congregation and I could work out together. Agreed we can't pray too much, just as we can't love too much. But we can have too many words of prayer. *In worship what matters is relationships, not words.* Jesus told us not to imagine that the more we say, the more likely we are to be heard (Matt. 6.7).

That leads me, thirdly, to ask afresh, What is worship for? That experience of mine beside the small lake in Wisconsin was meant to reconstruct from foundation to coping stone my theology—and also my worship. Conventional ideas need to be discarded.

Worship is like love. Worship is to give us time, first of

all, to become more aware of the wonder of God's love in Jesus, focussed on us. He who has seen Jesus and his loving has seen God and his loving of us. Next, our worship should express the response of our reawakened love to God. Then this love between God and ourselves, like all genuine love, should overflow—overflow on to those worshipping with us, our families, our friends, our neighbours and the world around us. Worship of this quality will not stunt us; rather it will help us to discover and to grow into our true selves. Let me make a small practical suggestion. Try always to arrive for worship five minutes early, then remember God's presence and reflect on what we are about to try to do. 'Much worship', a friend of mine, a bishop who goes to many churches, says, 'is spoilt before it starts.'

Fourthly, we are much too individualistic. So ingrained is our individualism that too often our worship consists of individuals saying synchronised prayers rather than a well-knit group of men and women really and deeply together praising God. We are called, as we have seen, to be a harmonious orchestra of love and praise to God, not a medley of individual musicians. When we come to worship, let us, then, besides remembering God's presence, take a quick look around and link ourselves in mind and heart with one another. As we grow in mutual understanding and love, so we grow in authentic praise and love to God.

INFORMAL PRAYING TOGETHER

Never do we pray alone. Whenever we pray, we pray in the Spirit of Jesus; and so we are one together in the Spirit. Dietrich Bonhoeffer used to pray every morning at six o'clock in his Nazi prison cell. He was aware that there and then he was one with his fiancée and with his aged parents. He tells them so in his letters. In my own prayers I too realise this invisible companionship. What a strength and joy it is.

So when we go to stay with friends who share our faith, what should be more natural to us than to pray together? But perhaps that cool reticence which some of us have inherited from early years may make us shy of sharing in this spontaneous prayer. Yet perhaps we could at least make a small beginning by being quiet together and praying slowly the Lord's prayer, or pondering together a psalm verse of thankfulness in gratitude for being together again. Let us not force the pace in our praying together; but we may soon find words of spontaneous prayer come to our lips.

I know what freshness and happiness have come in my life in many places where I have worked or visited, when small, unpressurised prayer-groups have emerged. Jesus spoke about two or three being 'gathered together in his name' for prayer. It is this spirit of intimate and heartfelt prayer that should overflow into and irrigate our large gatherings for worship.

It is said, 'You can't sing a love-song, unless you are in love'—or at least can't really sing it. Nor can we authentically sing the psalms and hymns of the Church or pray the great prayers of the Church, unless we have this love of the Lord in our hearts. I do not mean that we can expect always to feel deep emotion as we join together in the songs and prayers of the Church. As in human relationships, we go on being friends, loving one another, attending to one another, even at those times when we are not feeling much love. It is this deep-down love that holds us together and that keeps us faithful in our worship of God.

THE WORSHIP OF THE CHURCH AND THE HOLY COMMUNION

I wish I had time to glance at all the rich variety of the Church's worship. But I can only look at what most of us would see as the heart of our worship, the Holy Communion, the Lord's Supper, the Eucharist.

It means so much to me and to many of my friends —not because we happen to like it, but because Jesus himself has made it so central to us. 'Do this', he said, 'in remembrance of me.' Notice at what a moment he asked us to do this, on the night before Good Friday, just as he was going to consummate on the cross his life of never-ceasing love. And love is why we share in the Eucharist, our love responding to his love and to his request on that solemn night. 'Every participation in it', says Ruth Burrows, 'deepens our union with the Lord, a union which we must then live out in our everyday lives.'

The Eucharist should never lose its wonder for us. With its many facets it sparkles like a diamond. When before the Eucharist I kneel in prayer, I often think of the multitude of ways I have participated in it—on a log in a clearing of a forest in Malawi, on a flat rock at sunrise by the lake of Galilee with the water lapping at our feet, in a gem of a Norman church, in a fantastic, tall wooden cathedral in Guyana, in a packed monastic church in Zagorsk, in homes of my friends, in my study and in many college chapels.

Always different, ever the same. It is always, as Thomas à Kempis in *The Imitation of Christ* says, a double feast, 'a feasting on the Word of God and a feasting on the Bread of Life.' Through the liturgical movement in many of our churches we have begun to consider with more care the selection of our biblical readings in our worship and the wording of our prayers. I am glad, though I have a fear that sometimes we now think more of the words than of the One who comes. I am pleased too that many of us are going more frequently to Communion, but I have a similar fear that we sometimes take the Eucharist too much for granted, as we so easily take for granted the kindnesses of our partners and of our close and trusted friends. But we can't go to the Lord in the Eucharist too frequently, provided we go with wonder, love and thoughtfulness.

We can't always *feel* the presence of God with us in worship and prayer. But we should always remember and appreciate his presence. For this it is essential that we prepare beforehand. We should try to meditate at home on one of the scripture passages. We should think of whom we specially wish to bring into our intercessions. We should of course cleanse our hearts by repentance so

105

as to welcome the Risen Lord afresh into our daily lives.

At the quiet moment of Holy Communion Jesus gives himself to us and incorporates us into his offering of himself in love to the Father. 'In what you receive', Augustine says, 'you are offered.' As in all true love the receiving and giving become one. It is so good to be able to do all this in deep fellowship with our friends and fellow-believers at the Eucharist. It is sometimes difficult in human friendship to 'tear ourselves away' from someone we love. So we do not like to hurry away from these prayers of the Eucharist. And when we leave, we continue to give ourselves to God through Christ to serve in the world. That serving in the world we must look at next.

Yet wonderful as communal worship and the Eucharist can be, they are never enough by themselves. Our *personal* prayers are of irreplaceable importance, for they enrich and keep alive the worship of the Bride and Body of Christ. In the rule of that Taizé community, where communal worship, social action and personal prayer are so well integrated, Brother Roger has written: 'Corporate prayer does not dispense us from personal prayer. The one sustains the other. Let us each day take time to renew our personal intimacy with Jesus.'

> In all my praying let me remember others are praying.
> In the joy of loving let me remember the way is often steep.
> In all my serving let me learn how to get on with others.
> In the wonder of the Eucharist, let me renew my intimacy with Jesus.

9 ETERNAL LIFE AND SERVICE NOW

In the growing mutual confidence of friendship and love we help one another to discover and reveal who we actually are. The way is not always easy but we keep to it, because it is the road to maturing into our true selves. As the years go by, we realise there won't be time in this life to complete our mutual understanding and growing together.

This is perhaps what lies behind some words of Edward King, the much-beloved bishop for twenty-five years in the villages of Lincolnshire. At the college where I was trained for the ministry we still felt his warm influence, though it was many years ago that he had been principal there. He was something of a scholar and theologian. But people said his own self came out when, at the Lincoln county fair, he was chatting and laughing with the farmers and the men and their families, the stallholders and the youngsters in holiday mood. Once he wrote to a close friend: 'This world is where we make friendships; the world to come is where in a richer way we shall enjoy them.'

People nowadays speak more freely about death. I think of Dr Cecily Saunders' wonderful skill in preparing the dying and their families for this hour of departure. All this is part of our healthy concern for our complete selves, our body-and-spirit-in-one. Nor is this talk about death escapist; it does not divert our interest from the world of the present and our responsibilities in it—indeed rather the contrary.

LIFE BEYOND DEATH

I myself, perhaps foolishly, had seldom thought much about death. My life was packed with so much that was engrossing and enjoyable. Though newspapers were full of travelling accidents and violence, yet death looked only a distant hazard.

The possible nearness of death came home to me in an amusing and roundabout way. At that time I was teaching in a college and the rector of a country town asked me to preach the Three Hours' Service at midday on Good Friday. He called at the college and drove me to his church. In my address I of course spoke of Jesus' death and also of the uncertainty of our own lives. To make my point clearer, I said I had enjoyed my drive that morning, but no one could tell quite for certain whether I should arrive home alive. A broad smile went round the congregation. I didn't know what a brick I had dropped until after the service. Then in the vestry the rector said to me, 'I don't think you realised I've lately had my licence endorsed for dangerous driving.'

One thing is certain—we are going to die. What is it going to be like for us and for those dear to us? As a priest I have been at many death-beds; and it has sometimes been a wonderful experience for the dying person and for the rest of us. Of course let us admit we are naturally afraid of pain, of the unknown and of parting. There may be physical pain, but modern medicine can, I am told, usually make this bearable.

Next there is the unknown. Some people try to find assurance in psychical research or in other religious faiths. Personally I have now come to find the assurance I need in God and his love disclosed in Jesus. The eternal God has made me for himself, for an ever-deepening closeness to him. Paul discovered that nothing in this life could separate him from God's love in Jesus, and he was equally convinced that neither death could itself break this link of love (Rom. 8.38-39). But fundamentally my confidence rests in Jesus himself. As divine and human, he knows God, he knows us, he knows the potential relationships between God and ourselves in this world and in the life to come; and times without number he spoke of heaven.

Then there is the parting from those dear to us. But

already in this life we have experienced the tears of part-ings from one another for a time. We have discovered that even when we cannot see one another we are still close to one another. We are now certain that through the rhythm of parting and of being together again our love can be purified, sustained and enriched. We can understand the words of Francis de Sales to his dear friend Jeanne de Chantal: 'Nothing could possibly sepa-rate your soul from mine, the link is too strong; death itself cannot break it because it is fashioned from a subst-ance that lasts to all eternity.' Jesus himself confirms that this is so, when he said to the repentant thief dying on the cross beside him, 'Today shall you be with me in Para-dise.' They would be together and know that they were together.

WHAT IS HEAVEN?

On these grounds we can be sure of the life to come and of our being together there. The fact that we cannot de-scribe it does not make us any less certain of it. The words used by Jesus and the New Testament writers can-not be literal, descriptive words, because all our words have been coined to describe only the earthly experi-ence. So their words about heaven must be symbolic and illuminative. The streets of gold stand for an experience rich and glorious beyond anything we can think or im-agine. It will include the joy of being with our loved ones; and many of our misunderstandings will then be cleared up in the light of God's love. How we cannot say; but this is just another part of the inevitable limitations of our human language. An illustration may make all this clearer. A plane flew for the first time over a remote island in the Pacific. A Polynesian islander tried to de-scribe it. 'It was like a great bird,' he said, 'but it flew without flapping its wings and made the noise of a mil-lion bees.' That's the best he could do with his limited Polynesian vocabulary. But the fact that he could not describe the plane literally did not mean he was not sure whether he had seen it, still less that it was unreal.

What then is heaven? I would say that heaven is our continuing to grow in that friendship with God that we have begun to build up in this life. It begins here and goes deeper and deeper. 'This is eternal life,' we read in John's gospel, 'to know thee who alone art truly God, and Jesus Christ whom thou hast sent' (John 17.3).

Within this divine friendship we shall enter more deeply into our true human loves and friendships. 'We shall find them all in Him', C. S. Lewis wrote. 'By loving Him we shall love them more than we do now.' For all true love comes ultimately from God; now and in eternity, 'He who lives in love', the first letter of John says, 'lives in God' (1 John 4.16).

CARING WITHOUT BEING ANXIOUS

Yet in spite of all that we know about God and his unalterable love, we are naturally sometimes anxious about some who are close to us and others, too, for whom we have responsibility. They perhaps seem to have very little faith or to be living what appear to us to be careless lives.

God longs that all men and women should come to know him and so become their true selves. But he wishes them to come not through force, nor through fear, but through love. God does all that he can to attract them to himself. Yet if they are to come through love, God has to give them the freedom to choose, to respond to his love or not. Forced love is no love.

But it does no good to be anxious about them or their future. Our anxiety helps neither them nor us. In fact anxiety diminishes our vivacity and our chances of helping them. We must care and care deeply without being anxious.

Nor must we ever look down on them, nor judge them too severely. For once they sense this, we are cut off from almost any chance of helping them. 'Pass no premature judgement,' Paul says, 'for the Lord will bring to light what darkness hides, and disclose men's inward motives' (1 Cor. 4.5). Jesus himself told us that some of the prostitutes and dishonest tax-collectors are nearer to God than many of us who might consider ourselves religious (Matt. 21.31). Presumably this must be because they—in spite of harsh circumstances and inner 'blockages'—are seeking God more truly than some of us are. It may also well be that some people of other faiths or of no faith at all are responding more than we know to whatever light they are receiving. It is of course only through Jesus Christ—as the New Testament says—that all these people can come to God and to eternal joy. But many are helped by him without realising *who* it is who is helping them. John's gospel, you remember, tells us that Christ is the light who already lightens *every* man.

OUR RESPONSIBILITY—TOWARDS INDIVIDUALS AND TOWARDS SOCIETY

So God, disclosed in Jesus, is at work not only throughout the Church, but also far, far beyond it. As I travel in places as different as California and India— and as you go to your daily work—you and I must be training ourselves to look at each man, woman and child as someone precious, created in the image of God. In the heart of each one the love of God is already at work—perhaps obscurely—to help them to mature into their true selves. This maturity, as we have seen, can only come through ever-growing friendship both with God and with those around them. And this friendship, divine and human, begins and deepens here, but it can fully mature only in eternity. Winston Churchill once said, half in humour, 'There may be two worlds, but I prefer to deal with them one at a time.' I would say on the contrary that it is only in the light of our eternal destiny that we can see our full responsibilities towards one another in this world.

God does not do this work of bringing his sons and daughters to maturity, alone. He so deeply values and respects us that he asks us to be—in prayer and action— his collaborators, just as human hands collaborated to bring the blind and paralysed to Jesus for him to heal in body and in spirit.

111

Yet in our deep concern for others, we must not pressurise them. It puts them off. We must listen. We must respect what is good in their philosophies, faiths and cultures. But just as we share with them appropriate medical and educational skills, so equally we must train ourselves to offer to share our supreme spiritual treasure. The eternal Light, who lightens every man, has become man in Jesus our liberator. Not to share this is not to love.

We must be ready to do this in two ways—by helping individuals round about us and by trying to shape the wider society. I have said enough about the first way. I'll only add this, which links these two ways. It is no good saying we're concerned about the people of China or Afghanistan, if we are insensitive when we speak to people at work and in our shops and to the youngsters in our locality. This latter way tests the genuineness of the former.

What, then, about our influencing society? Society either helps or hinders us growing into our true selves. We all have to live in it. We either conform to its pressures or else react against them. None of us is untouched by it. So we who are deeply concerned with prayer and maturity cannot stand aside, uninvolved in society. Unfortunately because many of us can only do a little, we do in fact practically nothing.

At the very least we could raise these questions when we talk with our friends and colleagues. We should not 'opt out' of social and political issues. Jesus was not afraid of controversy in Nazareth. We can hardly complain of what others do in our professional associations or trades' unions, if we ourselves do nothing. I know it is difficult to make our voice heard; and it often takes a great deal of courage. And if we think our own voice won't count for much, could we look around to find others who share our concern? We can't campaign on every issue, because we must keep adequate time for our families and for recreation, for prayer and reflection. But we should keep an alert interest in what is going on in the world around us. *Humani nil a me alienum puto*

112

should be as true of any man or woman of prayer as it was of Terence the Latin poet—nothing that is human is outside my interest. Prayer does not narrow our concerns nor isolate us. If we can't do everything, ought we not to specialise in something, so that people can turn to us for an informed opinion at least on that subject? Ours should be no abstract interest. On this point at least I agree with Karl Marx. His words are engraved on his tombstone in the Highgate cemetery: 'Philosophers have only interpreted this world; the point however is that we must change it.' Though for us changing society is part of our loving, of our responding to God's love, seen in Jesus.

In passing I must add that often, when I have visited elderly housebound people and patients in hospital, I have come away myself refreshed not only by their cheerful courage but by their real outgoing concern. They are eager for discussion, keep themselves well informed, and so give themselves to God in daily prayer for the needs of the world. For them their concerned prayer is fruitful action.

My experience at the Wisconsin lake opened my eyes to the truth that, for me, my prayer cannot be authentic unless it leads me into action. Implementing this insight is going to mean a change in my style of life and ministry.

FOUR AREAS OF SPECIAL CONCERN

There are, I think, four interlinked areas of concern for our prayer and action—social, racial, ecological and international. This is fairly new ground at present for me. As you will see, I am at the stage of asking questions. In each area 'charity begins at home', as they say, but cannot end there. For us the immediate social problem in Britain is the millions of unemployed. What do we really know about it? Have we often talked with men and women now without a job, or with school-leavers without a job to go to? Do we know what it feels like? And what are its repercussions going to be? How can jobs be created, and soon? Even so, because of cheaper production abroad and higher technology at home, we are probably never going to know 'full employment' again. David Bleakley's book, *In Place of Work,* sets us thinking. But action is needed.

This leads us to discuss, What are we educating children and students for? How can we have academic excellence without social divisiveness? Why have statisticians so often got their figures wrong in the field of education? And when we look at our own localities, are there any particular groups of children whose needs are not being met? Are there pieces of constructive service young people could be engaged on?

Then our fresh understanding of ourselves as body-and-spirit-in-one raises questions about our medical service. Our hospitals are not factories in which damaged bodies are put in and repaired bodies come out as on a conveyor-belt. This raises questions about the training—and retraining—of doctors, nurses and paramedical personnel. Again, in the districts where we live, what about the hundreds of people who are struggling with personal and health problems? Their independence and personal dignity must be delicately respected. What help is there for families in tension, for people feeling inadequate, for lonely and ageing people? They are all created 'in the image of God', however much that gift and capacity may have been damaged. Jesus' parable of the good Samaritan tells me—and you—that high principles are not enough.

This brings us to our second major area of concern, the problems of race. Are poverty, and so violence, going to become inevitable both in particular localities and on a world scale? As we belong to the Body of Christ, a worldwide Church with all types of people, we ought to have something to say—and something to give. We remember Martin Luther King. How I wish his Christmas Eve message could always echo in our hearts: 'I still have a dream that one day every black in this country, every coloured person in the world, will be judged on the basis of the content of his character rather than the colour of his skin, and every man will *respect* the dignity and the worth of human personality.' How effective has his non-violence campaign proved in the long run to be? Does his assassination stand as a reminder to us that the patience of some is exhausted? What can be done to prevent violence spiralling into social disintegration? And what should our attitude be to the governments of the Right or the Left that maintain themselves through fear and the excessive use of force?

Thirdly, there is the ecological question. We are more aware now that we are using up the earth's limited resources far too fast—besides destroying so much of the beauty of the natural world. What makes it worse is the sight of over-production and reckless waste in some countries side by side with poverty and near-starvation in other countries. There may be other sources of energy yet to be tapped, but they will be limited and soon absorbed by the growth of world population. And may not newly-discovered resources be pillaged in the same reckless and unjust way? A. D. Lindsay, the Oxford scholar, who was always planning and working ahead of others, warned us a generation ago of our failure 'to harness the scientific mind to the merciful heart.' Unless some decisive action is taken soon, the unprincipled scramble for what is left of our resources may lead to widespread famine and to all but inevitable war.

Fourthly, looming over them all is the problem of international relationships and the danger of an escalating war. It is difficult to get at the truth in these matters. But do we really try to find out and to think things through, and see what it adds up to, irrespective of the propaganda from the Left or the Right? 'For evil to triumph it is enough for good men to keep silent.'

PRAYER AND ACTION

We cannot love God *or* our neighbour; we either love both or neither—so the first letter of John says. It then goes on to say our love must be 'not in word and talk, but in truth and in deed' (1 John 3.18). If we are men and women of authentic prayer, we are men and women of

115

loving action; though action, as we shall see in the next chapter, can without prayer become counterproductive.

Our action includes both helping others one by one to become their true selves, and also trying to change the social order. We must concentrate not on one or the other, but on both together. William Temple used to say to us: 'If we have to choose between making men Christians and making the social order more Christian, we must choose the former. But there is no such antithesis.'

So let us now as we come towards the end of our book try to commit ourselves in a fresh way to our daily prayer and action.

Help me, Lord, to reflect in silence on how *wonderful*
each man, woman and child is,
capable of friendship with you and with one another
in this world of today
and in life beyond this world.
Keep my ears and my heart open to their needs.
Help me through your Spirit now and every day
to think and pray, to decide and take action.

10 ROOTED AND GROUNDED IN LOVE

It was Alan Ecclestone, a priest for many years in a heavily-industrialised parish, a man deep in politics, who wrote: 'If we are not growing in prayer, we are not becoming mature human beings. We are leaving something undeveloped. God-given potentialities are being wasted.' It is not enough to be praying, it is a matter of *growing* in prayer. That does not mean leaving the world, withdrawing from our responsibilites of service.

SERVICE REQUIRES MATURITY

But haven't you noticed how much well-intentioned service fails to achieve its aims? This is something which must concern almost all of us; and it is very much linked with growing in prayer. In our service—whether it is teaching, caring for the sick or for those burdened with problems, bringing up a family or almost anything else—not only can we fail, but our service can even become counterproductive. Sometimes we can't quite see why we fail. And no one can always succeed. If you think about it, you will remember that even Jesus didn't always succeed. Yet we sometimes don't succeed because of one of two opposite but inter-related failings, though we are not always quite conscious of them.

The first is that we gradually get into the way of being self-assertive, over directive. 'Come along,' we say, 'just do it like this; can't you see?' This doesn't help others to think or to grow. They either follow passively, or else they resent it and perhaps rebel.

The second failing is that we become unduly diffident. We don't give clear directions at all. 'Times have changed,' we say, 'they won't take things in the old way'; and shrugging our shoulders we add, 'Let them learn for themselves, from their own mistakes.'

I know something about both of these failings myself. Both of them often come, if I may say so, from fear in our own hearts. We may be secretly afraid of those we are supposed to be helping. We may be afraid of losing our own carefully built up reputation. These fears come out of our own lack of personal security and maturity. And further, we cannot build up our own maturity: the only things we can build ourselves are flimsy facades to hide our real inner weakness.

Maturity grows of itself out of relationships, rich, trusting relationships with friends, partners and colleagues. We know what it's like to be understood, appreciated and loved by someone and how it helps us face life. Deep down we are steadier, stronger people. And in the same way, as we come to know the wonder of being understood by God himself, appreciated and unalterably loved by him, he becomes our 'strength' in all the pressures and ups and downs of life. Jesus' service stemmed from his deep relationship with God.

So one of our greatest assets in our responsibility of truly serving others is our growing intimacy and confidence not only in our friends, but in God himself. This means prayer, and growing in prayer. Carlo Carretto, one of the Little Brothers of Charles de Foucauld, writes that if we are deepening our prayer, 'it will be God Himself who will send us out, with greater strength, with greater love, towards others, so that we may love them more generously and serve them more sensitively.'

ABIDING IN CHRIST

Growing in prayer is not the same thing as having more frequent times of prayer. In fact I am not concerned with times of prayer, but I am concerned with praying, with praying without ceasing. Real praying, like loving, goes on all the time. Deep down, however engrossed we are in what we are doing, we are present to one another. Jordan of Saxony in his long journeys in the thirteenth century wrote to his beloved Diana d'Andalo: 'The more I realise how truly you love me from the depths of your soul, the more incapable I am of forgetting you and the more constantly are you in my thoughts.' When we are truly convinced of God's love for us in Jesus, how can we forget him? This is what Paul means when he speaks of 'Christ in you'; and what John means by our 'abiding in Christ' and 'abiding in his love'. Paul and John are not writing to a spiritual élite, but to husbands and wives, young people and old, to the ordinary run of Christians of their day.

The basic question for our maturity and service is just this: How can that unchangeable love of God, disclosed in Jesus, focussed on each one of us, become, as we say, 'part of ourselves'? How can we, deep down, *remain aware* of it, busy as we are? How can we say with Paul, 'the love of Christ directs us' in our daily lives?

When you are aware that someone loves you, you find all sorts of things remind you of the one who is always inwardly close to you. So it can be between the Lord and ourselves. You will find out for yourself what will remind you and link you with him in your everyday life. For me, when I sit down to a meal or see food being prepared, I am reminded of Jesus always coming to me in the eucharistic feast. A letter from a friend makes me think of the scriptures, in which Jesus so often comes to me. A knock at the door or the ring of the telephone brings back to me the time when I said 'Yes' to the Risen Jesus' call, 'Behold, I stand at the door and knock'. Flowers in a park or in the countryside or the sparkling stars at night speak to me of him:

I see his blood upon the rose,
　　And in the stars the glory of his eyes.

Deep love takes time to grow. We look back over the years we have known one another with deep gratitude. Paul speaks of our being 'rooted and grounded in love' (Eph. 3.17). John says we are branches *abiding* in Jesus the true vine. The rich sap rises from the roots and causes the branches to bear fruit. The fruit is not only love, joy and peace in our hearts; it is also the fruitfulness of the service to which we are sent; for Christ says not only that 'we shall bear fruit', but 'we shall *go* and bear fruit'. This can only be so, because we are in continual contact with Jesus, because we abide in him. Prayer is abiding.

Friends, lovers, partners know that if they are going to grow in love, they have to make time for one another. So if we are going to pray without ceasing, to abide continually in Jesus, to be rooted and grounded in love, we have to make time to be alone with him. We each have to find our own way to do this.

I and many of my friends have discovered we normally need two times a day. Let me try to explain. Human friendship and love requires a double rhythm of giving and receiving. We need to give our time, our thoughts, ourselves. No generous giving, no real friendship.

But if it is going to be authentic friendship, we must also be glad to receive; and some of us strangely find this more difficult. We must give up our excessive self-reliance and rejoice to be dependent. I do not mean an infantile dependence, but a joyful, adult dependence on one another. No glad dependence, no real friendship.

So in all friendship, human and divine, giving and receiving are interwoven. But in a certain sense receiving is primary. Love is a gift. This is specially so in our friendship with God in Christ. 'You did not choose me, but I chose you'; this is the mystery and wonder of our calling. It needs to be woven into the very fabric of our daily lives.

A DAILY QUIET TIME

I have found by experience, specially during these last few years, that I need daily a quiet time. This is the receiving side of my friendship with God. It is for me not primarily bible-study nor chiefly seeking guidance for my daily life. It is to open myself to God, disclosed in Jesus, to let myself be penetrated by his love. Unless I first receive his love into myself, I haven't much real love to share with others during the day. Jesus himself needed to find a quiet place for prayer very early each day (Mark 1.35). If he did, I know I do. I too need a special place of quiet and a special time. I keep in my room a small table with an open Bible and a picture, just as we have in our friendships places with special memories. And I have a special time quite early each morning. You may perhaps have to find some other time, but try to find a *daily* time. Though if we miss just once in a while, let us not be worried, as long as a steady relationship is being built up. But I know for myself if I start missing my daily quiet time, my sensitivity to others goes down, as I have said, and so does the quality of my writing and my work.

We each have to see what helps us most; but let me, so as to be brief and clear, tell you what I do. I am no expert. This is more or less a simplification of the bible-praying I wrote about in my chapter on the Holy Spirit. In many subjects, like mathematics, the further you go, the more complex it becomes. But in bible-praying the further you go, as in friendship, the simpler and deeper it becomes, and the fewer words you need.

The night before I normally read a very few verses usually from the gospels. These words simmer in my mind during the night. Then in the morning I do not have to waste precious time trying to find a suitable passage. My actual time of prayer is fairly unstructured and unpremeditated. Teresa of Avila said she did not know what she was going to say next to God, because it was love that spoke. Yet I have a rough mnemonic, *SARI*, whose letters form the initial letters of the four phases of my quiet prayer.

I begin with *stillness*. I normally sit, quiet, relaxed, remembering God's presence and asking the Spirit to help me in my prayer.

Then I *accept* God's love. To do this I often repeat quietly and slowly the passage I read the night before; this is not in order to learn more from it, but rather to hold myself quiet in the presence of the Lord. More simply at times I feel drawn to say again and again just a phrase, like 'My Lord and my God'; sometimes a single word is enough, like Jesus or Abba. This is, as we should expect, like human affection, when we say more than once, 'I love you' or we repeat the beloved's name.

Next, I try to *respond* to God's love. Sometimes I use words of my own or words that come to me spontaneously, like 'Jesus, my Lord, I thee adore; O make me love thee more and more.' Or sometimes my silence speaks more deeply to him than any words. This is by no means always an emotional experience. And often there are distracting thoughts; I try never to worry about them; sometimes the distraction leads me back to God; at other times I find it better to take no more notice of them than I do of the passing traffic outside my window. Beneath it all I know this accepting his love and responding is real. 'Abide in me and in my love.'

Finally I try to *intercede* a little. My main time for intercession is, as I will explain in a moment, later in the day. But I know this sharing of love between the Lord and myself must, because it is real, overflow to others. So I intercede for a few people who are close to me, or who have some great need that day. I pray that for them too love may grow, because that prayer includes all our true prayers. I finish by saying the Lord's prayer slowly, asking that the kingdom of God's love may spread throughout the world.

I usually jot down in my private spiritual journal a few words of scripture so that it will go on sounding in my ears during the day, as Dietrich Bonhoeffer put it: 'just like the words of someone you love.' Sometimes I add a brief reflection of my own. Then to look at this little log-book day by day, week by week, is often quite an encouragement, especially when life's journey becomes steep. And I try never to hurry away from prayer, any more than I would from a close friend.

SHARING THE DAY WITH THE LORD

I certainly need another time of prayer for the giving side of my friendship with God, a time when I can place my daily concerns in the Lord's hands. I used to do this last thing at night, and I still need a few minutes of sincere, trustful prayer then. But I know now that for this giving prayer I need to arrange for at least a quarter of an hour in the late afternoon or early evening. I may lose a quarter of an hour's work, but the work I do after my prayer is more lively work and more related to people. Father Basil Pennington, the American Cistercian guide to prayer, requires all who come to him regularly for his advice to give twenty minutes to prayer twice a day. This, he says, is their sign that they seriously wish to grow in love and prayer. We should aim at this plan if we are really going to discover our true selves through this friendship with God.

My evening prayer is spontaneous, like a real conversation. But to prevent my forgetting anything important, I usually follow a kind of sequence. For this also I have a mnemonic, *ARTIST*: its six letters stand again for the names of the six steps of my prayer.

If you should not feel in the mood for prayer—and this happens to all of us—you could read slowly a few suitable verses from the Bible or from some book on prayer that appeals to you. That often helps, but don't be led on to read too much. This is the time for praying, not for reading. I always begin my prayers—by saying nothing. I relax, I realise the presence of God and his love, I ask the Holy Spirit to help me to pray and to mean it. I don't begin by speaking to God about my problems or the troubles of the world. When a friend calls to see us, we look into his eyes: 'How glad I am to see you', we say.

So it is in prayer. I begin by, as it were, looking at God with wonder and love. This is what I mean by *adoration*. There are many ways of doing this. On some days I remember God's coming to us in Jesus. So I ponder—I don't picture details—on, for example, how Jesus came in love and mystery to the lakeside, when the disciples had gone back to their fishing after his resurrection. And I'm glad he is equally with me—'the same yesterday, today and for ever.' On other days I begin my prayer by enjoying again the beauty of his creation seen on my holidays—a holiday photograph in the pages of my Bible is often quite a help and inspiration—or the beauty of the garden and trees outside my window; and so I lift my heart to him in praise. Or at other times I quietly remind myself that we live *in* him and that his love enfolds us like the air we breathe—'In him we live and move, in him we exist'—and I rejoice in the wonder of his presence and love. We find out which of the many ways helps us most, and it varies from day to day. But it is adoration which leads into prayer.

When we are aware of God's presence and goodness and love, we can't help being sorry for the many times we must have disappointed him and so we apologise and *repent*. There is nothing forced about this and it happens practically spontaneously. And how relieved we are to be still and to receive his forgiveness.

This leads us on to *thanking* God. How very much we are grateful for, even amongst all the more perplexing things of life! It is daily appreciation and gratitude which keeps fresh both our human relationships and our friendship with God.

Our gratitude for all that God has done for us, and for all that our friends have done for us, inspires us to *intercede* for others. How good it is towards the end of the day to bring our friends in our hearts to God. He has through Jesus drawn us so close to himself and in his love so close to one another. Because we love, we pray. However far apart we may be, we know we are one *in* him. With them we also bring others trustfully to him, those whose joys and confidences we have shared, and those for whom we have some responsibility. And so our intercession fans out.

We must leave time for prayer for *self*. What a blessing it is to have some human friend we can speak to spontaneously about our achievements and our fears, who won't then think us 'uppish' or weak, but who will just understand us. This helps us to drop the defences that our superficial external self puts up and so we grow towards our true selves. What a relief it is each evening to speak also to God like that! Of course he knows already what is going on inside us, but it is in this way that we grow towards what he wants us to be, his confident and open friends.

This helps us to know both our gifts and our gaps. Let us discover and develop all our gifts. Even so, if we rely only on our own resources and our own sensitivity, we cannot do our best for others. How can we really help others, unless we talk over with God our daily contacts with them? It is through this daily talking with him that we gradually grasp how true it is that without Jesus, the true vine, we can—on the deepest level—do nothing for them.

This leads us naturally to the last part of our prayer, *trust*. The more we try to enter into the problems of those round about us, the more sensitive we become to the complexities of our world, the more we are in danger of being overwhelmed, even disorientated, by it all. So at the end of our evening prayer we need to rest trustfully in the Lord. Mother Julian, that woman of deep prayer in mediaeval Norwich, wrote in her autobiographical *Revelations of Divine Love*: 'God said not "You shall not be tempested", but "You shall not be overcome." ' Paul too knew that he could not in his own resources weather all the hardships and pressures of his life, but he discovered 'I have strength for anything *in him* who gives me power' (Phil. 4.13). How good it is to sum up our evening prayer by quietly, and perhaps repeatedly, saying such affirmations of deep trust in God, and making them our own. Love frequently expressed is the love that grows. So it is also with trust.

A FRESH STAGE

Now I have shared with you what have been my discoveries since that day beside the small Wisconsin lake. So as I am writing these closing pages, I am praying for you and for myself as we set out together with confidence, love and openness on a new stage of our journey with all the freshness of a new start. I am very conscious of my own need to find out still more who I am, so that I can best carry out the wonderful calling and responsibilities God has given to me. I shall need—as you will—all the encouragement available. Paul said, 'I press on, reaching out for what lies ahead'. We need to travel light. God does not mean us to be burdened with a mass of rules. Jesus loved and lived and died to liberate us from that. Let us choose what helps we need and keep to them.

One of the joys of my life is that it brings me real friends in many countries and I am often invited to stay with wonderful people. Some of the most wonderful have been old couples. I remember one marvellous old couple as vividly as if it all happened yesterday. When I arrived, they said something like this: 'You're very, very welcome. We're getting a bit slow and arthritic, but we'll do our best to look after you.' They said rather apologetically, 'their best'; but I have never been so well cared for, so well understood; they seemed to have developed a 'sixth sense' of love.

Seldom have I seen such love. It is the same tender love that they had had when they first really knew one another and set up home together. It is not a thinner, tired kind of love. It is the same warm love—tested, deepened, enriched and overflowing. They had for so long been so close that they understood one another—and me—intuitively. Words were hardly needed. Their love was so perceptive. It was the real thing. They told me about their life together. They had shared such a variety of experiences: marvellous holidays and other high moments; some uneventful, dull patches and without much money; sickness and problems, even in their own happy family circle. And—nearly all couples have them—some inexplicable dark times, when they could not understand or even hardly talk to one another. But it was by working through *all* these experiences together that they had come to discover their true selves and to grow into real depth of mutual love and so could make their love a joy and strength for others.

And so it is with our love for one another and for God. We are on an enchanting journey, but an all-weather journey. Yet I have found many more fresh spring days than I expected. But we must put down deep roots. We need deep roots in daily prayer, abiding in him, rooted and grounded in love. So year by year we shall help one another to discover and to grow into our true selves, into the true humanness we see in Jesus. And we shall never—here or in eternity—cease to wonder that we are loved with that love we see disclosed in Jesus.

'He who has seen me has seen the Father'.
In quietness and in confidence shall be your strength.
Abba, Father, thank you for disclosing to us in Jesus
  both your own self and your eternal love for us
  and also the men and women you call us to be.
Thank you that through Jesus you set us free to be-
                                come our true selves
  and so through your Spirit to love and serve the
                                world around us.
Help us to press forward,
  abiding in Christ, the true vine, by love and prayer
                                now and for ever.

FOR FURTHER READING

L. Boff, *Jesus Christ Liberator*, SPCK, 1980

R. Burrows, *To Believe in Jesus*, Sheed and Ward, 1978

C. H. Dodd, *The Founder of Christianity*, Fount, 1973

J. D. G. Dunn, *Jesus and the Spirit*, SCM Press, 1975

A. Ecclestone, *Yes to God*, Darton, Longman and Todd, 1975

A. T. and R. P. C. Hanson, *Reasonable Belief*, Oxford University Press, 1980

R. Harries, *Being a Christian*, Mowbray, 1981

P. Hinchliff and D. Young, *The Human Potential*, Darton, Longman and Todd, 1981

H. Küng, *On Being a Christian*, Fount, 1978

D. W. D. Shaw, *Who is God?*, SCM Press, 1968

J. Sobrino, *Christology at the Crossroads*, SCM Press, 1978

W. H. Vanstone, *Love's Endeavour, Love's Expense*, Darton, Longman and Todd, 1977

J. N. Ward, *The Use of Praying*, Epworth, 1967